I0817288

PRAY WITH JESUS

A PRAYER BOOK FOR WOMEN

PRAY WITH JESUS

A PRAYER BOOK FOR WOMEN

A Year of Daily Scriptures and Prayers for Everyday Faith

ALEXIS KANODE

Z FAITH • NEW YORK

Z Faith
An imprint of Zeitgeist™
A division of Penguin Random House LLC
1745 Broadway, New York, NY 10019
zeitgeistpublishing.com
penguinrandomhouse.com

ISBN: 9798217151110
Ebook ISBN: 9798217151103

Printed in the United States of America
1st Printing

Illustrations © by Shutterstock.com/Great Bergens
Book design by Emma Hall
Edited by Caroline Lee

The authorized representative in the EU for product safety and compliance is Penguin Random House Ireland, Morrison Chambers, 32 Nassau Street, Dublin D02 YH68, Ireland. https://eu-contact.penguin.ie

This prayer book is for every woman longing for a deeper relationship with Christ, trusting God with every dream and desire, and seeking to glorify Him.

INTRODUCTION

Prayer wasn't always part of my daily routine. Before I knew Jesus personally, I didn't understand why prayer was important or even how to pray. Prayer was something I only did in moments of crisis.

When I came to know the love of Christ in college at the age of 19, I was so overwhelmed by his love, grace, and mercy. I was eager to dive headfirst into getting to know God deeply and personally. I learned that Jesus, the Son of God, made prayer a priority. If Jesus needed prayer, how much more do we?

After experiencing prayer as a constant open line of communication with the Lord, I don't know how I ever lived without it. Sometimes, it looks like asking God for help, provision, and breakthrough. Other times, it's coming to him with gratitude for all he's done. As a mom of two, it's hard to find the perfect moment to pray. But God is always willing to meet me in the raw, messy, and honest moments of prayer. It's often there that I encounter his deep love, power, comfort, and guidance.

No matter where you are in your journey, I pray you experience God's grace, power, and love through the 365 prayers and Scriptures in this book. Whether you're reading it from beginning to end, flipping through to find prayers that speak to you, or seeking encouragement in a challenging season—however you use it, I hope it will strengthen your faith and draw you closer to the Lord.

PRAYER IS A DIRECT LINE TO THE LORD

In the Old Testament, priests had to travel great distances to get to the Tabernacle or the Temple and only the high priest had access to the most sacred place, the Holy of Holies, once a year, to have a direct line of communication with the Lord. The Holy of Holies was separated by a thick curtain—what was referred to as the veil. When Jesus died on the cross, he not only took our sin upon himself, but he also tore the veil.

The significance of the veil being torn is, we now have a direct line to our heavenly Father through Jesus. Jesus tore the veil in two upon his death, signifying that we now have the privilege of having direct and constant communication with our heavenly Father.

Jesus taught us that prayer doesn't need to be fancy, it doesn't need to be long and drawn out, and it shouldn't cause confusion. Matthew 6:7 tells us, "And when you pray, do not use vain repetitions as the heathen *do*. For they think that they will be heard for their many words." He is saying we simply need to just come to the Lord in prayer with a sincere heart (Hebrews 10:22).

The most uplifting thing to me about prayer is, there is no one way to pray. We are able to pray short, quick prayers, such as, "Lord, help me." We are also able to pray in great detail for something. I take comfort in knowing God already knows my heart and my innermost thoughts, but he also wants to hear from me.

Just as I love to hear my kids babble as babies and have conversations with them as they grow, God is the same with us. He longs to hear from us, he has a desire for us to draw near to him, and in turn, he draws near to us (Jeremiah 29:13).

There are times when we simply aren't sure how to pray, or we just don't have the words ourselves. I pray this book helps with that. It is my prayer that this book will equip you with the words to say when you just don't know what to say. I pray this book fosters your own prayer life and encourages you to pray consistently, talking to your heavenly Father about anything and everything that happens throughout your day.

We are blessed to have this open invitation with our heavenly Father because of what Jesus did on the cross. My hope is that this book can offer a bridge to help you grow toward a constant conversation with God in your everyday life. So let's walk this bridge together, toward growth in our relationship with Christ through the increase of our prayer life.

DAY 1

He Knows Me

God knew me before I was born.

But when it pleased God, who separated me from my mother's womb and called *me* through His grace, to reveal His Son in me, that I might preach Him among the Gentiles, I did not immediately confer with flesh and blood.

—GALATIANS 1:15–16

Dear God, you created me with care, shaping every part of who I am. Before I was born, you knew me and designed a purpose that is uniquely mine. Thank you for calling me to follow Jesus in a way that uses the gifts you've placed in me. Whether I'm at work, home, or anywhere in between, help me walk boldly in that calling, trusting that no moment is too insignificant to show your love. Let your Spirit guide me to live out the special story you've written for my life. In Jesus's name, amen.

DAY 2

Provision

If I seek God first, I will be given everything I need.

"Therefore do not worry, saying, 'What shall we eat?' or 'What shall we drink?' or 'What shall we wear?' For after all these things the Gentiles seek. For your heavenly Father knows that you need all these things. But seek first the kingdom of God and His righteousness, and all these things shall be added to you. . . ."

—MATTHEW 6:31–33

Dear heavenly Father, with each new day, my mind is busy trying to be productive or maximize my time, and I run scrambling to find solutions. I choose now to seek you—to stop worrying about my needs because you always provide. When I stop stressing about my plans, you can work in my life and everything can fall into place. In Jesus's name, amen.

DAY 3

The Light of the World

Forever thankful for the light of life.

Then Jesus spoke to them again, saying, "I am the light of the world. He who follows Me shall not walk in darkness, but have the light of life."

—JOHN 8:12

Dear Father God, your light exposes darkness, so we are no longer in fear. Because of Jesus's sacrifice on the cross, I am no longer ruled by worry and shame. As the light of the world, you offer the promise of healing and restoration. Thank you for Jesus's light of life that lives in me. Grow this light brighter in me every single day. In Jesus's name, amen.

DAY 4

Magnify His Name

Christ will be magnified through me.

For I know that this will turn out for my deliverance through your prayer and the supply of the Spirit of Jesus Christ, according to my earnest expectation and hope that in nothing I shall be ashamed, but with all boldness, as always, so now also Christ will be magnified in my body, whether by life or by death.

—PHILIPPIANS 1:19-20

Dear God, refine in me the same mindset as Paul, a fully surrendered heart and a commitment to glorifying you in all things. Help me live with the same conviction and a boldness to share at any time why my hope is in Jesus. The eternal hope I have in you shines through me as a reminder to others that true freedom is found in Christ alone. In Jesus's name, amen.

DAY 5

More Precious than Rubies

I have freedom as a daughter in Christ.

And He said to her, "Daughter, your faith has made you well. Go in peace, and be healed of your affliction."

—MARK 5:34

Dear Jesus, I want to become the daughter God created me to be. When the desperate woman touched your garment, you felt her belief and knew her suffering. Despite the demands for your attention and healing from the crowd, you stopped in that moment and chose to make a sacred space for her with your time and care. You freed her from her physical suffering but also in her spirit. You claimed her as your daughter, gave her a place to rest, restored her, and gave her access to you. I feel complete and wholly satisfied to know that this is true for me, too. In your name, amen.

DAY 6

Fervent Prayer Life

I long for a rich prayer life—with just the Lord and me.

But you, when you pray, go into your room, and when you have shut your door, pray to your Father who *is* in the secret *place*; and your Father who sees in secret will reward you openly.

—MATTHEW 6:6

Dear Lord, keep me consistent in spending time in your word. Like Jesus, I long for a vibrant prayer life where I can enter your presence and clearly hear your voice. The busyness of life can distract me from prioritizing prayer, so train my heart to seek you above all else. Teach me to enter the secret place as Jesus always did, to quiet and refresh my soul. In Jesus's name, amen.

DAY 7

Continuous Prayer

The will of the Lord is for me to pray without ceasing.

Rejoice always, pray without ceasing, in everything give thanks; for this is the will of God in Christ Jesus for you.

—1 THESSALONIANS 5:16–18

Dear heavenly Father, you encourage me to be in constant prayer and thanksgiving to and with you throughout my day. Make prayer my first response, rather than a last resort; not just in the difficult times, or only in my quiet times with you. I want to give you my first thoughts, not the leftovers. In Jesus's name, amen.

DAY 8

Rest for the Weary Soul

I find rest and peace in the comfort of my heavenly Father.

Come to Me, all *you* who labor and are heavy laden, and I will give you rest.

—MATTHEW 11:28

Dear God, the demands of life and the weight of juggling everything gets heavy, but when I believe your promises, I can truly rest, not just for my physical body, but for my soul. Trusting your plans, knowing I'm safe with you, and being certain you'll take care of my every need gives me the safety I seek. When life feels overwhelming, you provide the peace I need. In Jesus's name, amen.

DAY 9

Mustard Seed Faith

A faith that can move mountains.

So Jesus said to them, "Because of your unbelief; for assuredly, I say to you, if you have faith as a mustard seed, you will say to this mountain, 'Move from here to there,' and it will move; and nothing will be impossible for you. However, this kind does not go out except by prayer and fasting."

—MATTHEW 17:20-21

Dear Jesus, sometimes I'm filled with fear and have only a tiny bit of faith. Yet even then, you've shown up and worked miracles in my life. Faith is not the absence of fear but choosing to trust you in the midst of it. You meet me where I am, and you pursue a personal connection with me and I am not alone. Grow my faith until I believe wholeheartedly that nothing is impossible for you. In your name, amen.

DAY 10

Spirit of Unity

The Holy Spirit inspires and brings his people together.

And suddenly there came a sound from heaven, as of a rushing mighty wind, and it filled the whole house where they were sitting. Then there appeared to them divided tongues, as of fire, and *one* sat upon each of them. And they were all filled with the Holy Spirit and began to speak with other tongues, as the Spirit gave them utterance.

—ACTS 2:2-4

Dear heavenly Father, you never intended for my faith journey to be walked alone, we are not meant to be Christians in isolation. Surround me with others who also love you deeply. Delight in us when we come together in fellowship with one another. As I gather with my faithful brothers and sisters, knit our hearts together so that we are unified by your Spirit and love. In Jesus's name, amen.

DAY 11

Merciful Father

God delights in mercy.

But God, who is rich in mercy, because of His great love with which He loved us, even when we were dead in trespasses, made us alive together with Christ (by grace you have been saved) . . .

—EPHESIANS 2:4–5

Dear merciful and gracious Father, your mercy means I receive what I don't deserve. Not only do I simply receive your love, but through Jesus, I receive an eternal, free flow of it. Your pure objective to love comes at no cost to accept, which is counter to what I can expect in a world that values transactions. Thank you and in Jesus's name I pray, amen.

DAY 12

Overcoming Strife

Jealousy is from my flesh, not spirit.

"So he answered and said to *his* father, 'Lo, these many years I have been serving you; I never transgressed your commandment at any time; and yet you never gave me a young goat, that I might make merry with my friends. But as soon as this son of yours came, who has devoured your livelihood with harlots, you killed the fatted calf for him.'

"And he said to him, 'Son, you are always with me, and all that I have is yours.' "

—LUKE 15:29–31

Dear Lord, I foolishly fall for thinking traps that snare me and stir up friction, either within myself or with others. My resentments, jealousy, or clashing perspectives all scheme to insist on my way. The older brother in the parable of the prodigal son wanted recognition for his filial contributions and ultimately isolates himself from his family. When I feel my own defenses rise up inside of me and stir up division in my personal relationships, give me a heart to return and lean on your Spirit. Refine me to be spiritually mature; you are always near to hear my distress. In Jesus's name, amen.

DAY 13

Love in Action

Help me notice the needs of others.

"So which of these three do you think was neighbor to him who fell among the thieves?"

And he said, "He who showed mercy on him."

Then Jesus said to him, "Go and do likewise."

—LUKE 10:36-37

Dear Father God, you call me to love as you do, not just in words but in action. Help me live out a love that goes beyond comfort and convenience. Show me what it looks like to love sacrificially. Grow in me a genuine interest in the well-being of others; help me notice the needs of others and respond with care like the Good Samaritan who helped a stranger without expecting anything in return. Help me be someone others can count on and trust. In Jesus's beautiful name, amen.

DAY 14

Servant Leadership

Create in me a servant leader.

"Yet it shall not be so among you; but whoever desires to become great among you, let him be your servant."

—MATTHEW 20:26

Dear Lord, in your kingdom, leadership is being in the position of a servant, not someone of high status. Compared to the world's ways, your kingdom is upside down: The greatest are the least and the least are the greatest. Jesus knelt to wash the feet of his disciples when they could have been washing his. Give me Jesus's willing and selfless heart to serve. When you call me to lead, let me walk with humility, sacrifice, and love. In Jesus's name, amen.

DAY 15

Contentment over Comparison

I want a heart fixed on Jesus, not on what I don't have.

A sound heart *is* life to the body,
But envy *is* rottenness to the bones.

—PROVERBS 14:30

Dear Father God, guard my heart from envy. When I lust after more financial security, recognition for my contributions, or a more comfortable life, give me the wisdom to catch myself quickly and replace it with gratitude. I give thanks for the gift of ambition so that I may fuel and redirect that energy to serve you with purpose and passion. Anchor me in the truth: Your plans are tailor-made for me, and I don't need to compare my lot with anyone else's. The life you offer is abundant for me, and I can celebrate others' blessings and always walk in love. In Jesus's name, amen.

DAY 16

Help Me Love Well

Help me to be a friend who can give love generously.

A friend loves at all times,
And a brother is born for adversity.

—PROVERBS 17:17

Dear Father God, putting my trust in others and vulnerably showing my flaws feels like a big risk. But you have given us the beautiful gift of friendship. Give me the courage to ask for support when I need it so I can experience the joy and richness of walking and growing with those you've placed in my life. Nurture me to also to be a steadfast figure to those I love, someone who can show up with love, and with the ability to put their needs before my own, just as Jesus did. In Jesus's name, amen.

DAY 17

He Came to Call Sinners

Guard me from the sin of self-righteousness.

And when the scribes and Pharisees saw Him eating with the tax collectors and sinners, they said to His disciples, "How *is it* that He eats and drinks with tax collectors and sinners?"

—MARK 2:16

Dear Jesus, you sat with the people that society rejected and labeled as the worst sinners. You challenged the self-righteous who believed their good deeds made them better than others. Protect my heart from that kind of pride and hypocrisy. Help me never assume I'm better than someone else because their sin looks different than mine. You call everyone to repentance. In your name, amen.

DAY 18

Walk in Integrity

Integrity is security.

He who walks with integrity walks securely,
But he who perverts his ways will become known.

—PROVERBS 10:9

Dear heavenly Father, let me be the same person in front of others as I am when no one is looking so that I can be free to be myself in any scenario. When I make the right choices in you, I'm aligned with you, which is the ultimate confidence to represent Jesus through my life. Will you give me the security I need today so I won't fear being true to who you made me to be? In Jesus's name, amen.

DAY 19

Chosen to Be Fruitful

God has chosen and appointed me.

You did not choose Me, but I chose you and appointed you that you should go and bear fruit, and *that* your fruit should remain, that whatever you ask the Father in My name He may give you.

—JOHN 15:16

Dear Lord, like a branch depends on the vine, I need to stay connected to you. You are my source of life and purpose and without you, I am so limited in doing what truly matters or producing anything that lasts. Keep me close and connected to you so everything I do flows from you. In Jesus's name, amen.

DAY 20

Protect Your Peace

I want to protect my peace.

And let the peace of God rule in your hearts, to which also you were called in one body; and be thankful.

—COLOSSIANS 3:15

Dear Father God, there's so much noise around me. Fear, comparison, distraction; all try to steal the peace you've given me. Like Mary, who chose to sit at Jesus's feet while Martha was overwhelmed, help me choose what truly matters. Your peace guards my heart and mind when I stay close to you. Transform my heart to protect the peace you've placed within me. Thank you for being my safe place. In Jesus's name, amen.

DAY 21

Listening to Wise Counsel

God has provided wisdom through relationships.

The way of a fool *is* right in his own eyes,
But he who heeds counsel *is* wise.

—PROVERBS 12:15

Dear God, when I think I'm always right, pride blinds me to the ways you're trying to grow me. Thank you for the teachers and lessons I encounter to reveal my blind spots. Thank you for surrounding me with wise people who speak truth into my life. You bring the right voices at always the right time. Soften my heart to consider feedback without defensiveness, to know what to take to heart and what to release. In Jesus's name, amen.

DAY 22

Grace Changes Everything

God's strength is perfected in my weakness.

And He said to me, "My grace is sufficient for you, for My strength is made perfect in weakness." Therefore most gladly I will rather boast in my infirmities, that the power of Christ may rest upon me.

—2 CORINTHIANS 12:9

Dear Father God, I long to see your grace powerfully work in my life, especially through my shortcomings. Please transform my weaknesses into strengths. When I stumble, don't let me forget that your grace is a gift because you love me, not something I earn through performance. It's only by your power alone that I can boldly step forward in your path for me. In Jesus's name, amen.

DAY 23

Refined in the Fire

Purify me and create in me a clean heart.

Beloved, do not think it strange concerning the fiery trial which is to try you, as though some strange thing happened to you; but rejoice to the extent that you partake of Christ's sufferings, that when His glory is revealed, you may also be glad with exceeding joy.

—1 PETER 4:12–13

Dear Lord, becoming more Christlike is full of trials, and the refining fire is anything but comfortable. But I know you're doing a deeper work in me. You're testing and cementing my faith, working on my attitude, and revealing what needs to be healed, surrendered, and released. Every hardship produces something valuable in me: endurance, character, and hope. Like gold refined in fire, purify me so that when others look at me, they see your reflection shining in me. In Jesus's name, amen.

DAY 24

A New Thing

God will give me my breakthrough.

Behold, I will do a new thing,
Now it shall spring forth;
Shall you not know it?
I will even make a road in the wilderness
And rivers in the desert.

—ISAIAH 43:19

Dear God, you are the God who can do all things. You provide grander options in my life. When it feels like I am stuck, I can turn to you and trust you to take me out of the wild. You are faithful to make a way where there is no way—you make roads in the wilderness and rivers of water in the desert. Thank you for doing the impossible in my life. In Jesus's name, amen.

DAY 25

Faith in the Waiting

I have the hope that God always hears me.

Therefore I will look to the Lord;
I will wait for the God of my salvation;
My God will hear me.

—MICAH 7:7

Dear Lord, I bring you my prayers but sometimes the silence lingers. I feel alone to figure things out on my own and I question if you really hear me. Like a child, I expect you to immediately meet my every demand. You ask me to wait on an answer or sometimes your answer is no. Even when I don't see change or immediate developments, I want to take comfort in knowing that you are listening and love me. Please wipe any doubt that is hiding in my heart. In Jesus's name, amen.

DAY 26

My Refuge

God is good and trustworthy.

The Lord *is* good,
A stronghold in the day of trouble;
and He knows those who trust in Him.

—NAHUM 1:7

Dear God, you are my refuge and fortress of protection in every storm. In your arms, I'm completely safe. I bring all my fears to you because you are always there when I need you. Thank you for the security of your constant presence. Whenever I'm in a bind and I'm tempted to fix everything myself, remind me that you are my deliverer. In Jesus's name, amen.

DAY 27

Radiant Gratitude

Give me gratitude and a rejoicing heart.

"For my eyes have seen Your salvation
Which You have prepared before the face of all peoples,
A light to *bring* revelation to the Gentiles,
And the glory of Your people Israel."

—LUKE 2:30–32

Dear Jesus, Simeon believed and waited for your birth and arrival. When he finally encountered you as an infant, he sang your praises! Even as Simeon waited, he understood that God fulfills his promise. Give me the same radiant gratitude and a rejoicing heart because even when circumstances are unresolved, gratitude, hope, and joy can still be found from simply encountering your presence. I am joyful because I know you. In your name, amen.

DAY 28

Accept This Offering

I can always be an example of godliness.

Let no one despise your youth, but be an example to the believers in word, in conduct, in love, in spirit, in faith, in purity.

—1 TIMOTHY 4:12

Dear God, I sometimes wonder if my efforts matter, as it seems there is always someone to do it better. But when I experience you through all of your creation, your design in everything with microscopic detail tells me that I am placed exactly where you call me to be. My efforts don't need to shake the world, I can bless your name through ordinary moments, whether it's as an active member in my community or to spread joy and laughter with loved ones. Give me an earnest attitude because it doesn't go unnoticed by you. I give you what is uniquely mine and come sit at your feet with complete devotion. In Jesus's name, amen.

DAY 29

Trusting God's Direction

Look to God in everything.

In all your ways acknowledge Him,
And He shall direct your paths.

—PROVERBS 3:6

Dear heavenly Father, so many decisions wait for me each day, which tasks to tackle first or how to answer an email. I want the certainty of making the best and wisest choices, but you ask me to simply trust you. If I simply look to you, the demands suddenly look smaller and the urgency to achieve fades. Guide each of my decisions. Lead me through my day and direct my path. In Jesus's name, amen.

DAY 30

Seeking Your Counsel

I want to choose humility over pride.

When pride comes, then comes shame;
But with the humble *is* wisdom.

—PROVERBS 11:2

Heavenly Father, guard me from the tendency to rely on my own insight and human wisdom. King Saul's pride led him to press ahead on his own timing and give in to pressures to make a sacrifice before battle without waiting on your guidance. Teach me instead to be more like David, who sought you before acting and found protection and victory in battle. Keep my heart humble and quick to pray, knowing that you are always there to hear and guide my ideas. In Jesus's name, amen.

DAY 31

Renewed

I want to look like God, not the world.

And do not be conformed to this world, but be transformed by the renewing of your mind, that you may prove what *is* that good and acceptable and perfect will of God.

—ROMANS 12:2

Dear Abba Father, you have set me apart for a special purpose and have called me to look different than the rest of the world. Thank you for never giving up on me so I can know you deeply as you change my heart day by day. Renew my mind with your word. In Jesus's name, amen.

DAY 32

Honest Confession

I am safe to honestly confess all things to God.

"And you shall know the truth, and the truth shall make you free."

—JOHN 8:32

Dear Lord, you invite me to tell you my deepest fears and struggles. You want me to bring the parts of me that I hide from others. When I bury guilt, sin, mistakes, or shame, I can't fully receive your healing. Shine your light on everything I've tried to stifle so it no longer has power over me. You always meet my honest confession with grace and mercy, not condemnation, and this is where true freedom begins. In Jesus's loving name, amen.

DAY 33

He Is with Me

God will dwell with us in the flesh for eternity.

And I heard a loud voice from heaven saying, "Behold, the tabernacle of God *is* with men, and He will dwell with them, and they shall be His people. God himself will be with them *and be* their God."

—REVELATION 21:3

Dear God, I love being in your presence, and am thankful you have chosen to dwell with me! When I am worn and depleted, you give me shelter to rest. You sent your Son to be among the people to give them a path toward you. Through Jesus, you gave us a safe place on earth and when he showed radical humility, he gave us a way to true and perfect peace. Thank you. In Jesus's name, amen.

DAY 34

Mountain-Moving Faith

I want blind faith.

Now faith is the substance of things hoped for, the evidence of things not seen.

—HEBREWS 11:1

Dear heavenly Father, stretch my faith so I can trust you to move mountains even when prayers go unanswered or don't turn out the way I hope. Give me an unwavering faith like Shadrach, Meshach, and Abendego, who knew they'd be safe in the fiery furnace, because you were right there with them (Daniel 3:16–25). When doubt or uncertainty creeps into my heart, I thank you for always being faithful. In Jesus's name, amen.

DAY 35

No Comparison

There is only one of me.

For we dare not class ourselves or compare ourselves with those who commend themselves. But they, measuring themselves by themselves, and comparing themselves among themselves, are not wise.

—2 CORINTHIANS 10:12

Dear heavenly Father, you made me with the exact gifts, traits, and skills for the unique calling you've placed on my life. Humble me to understand it's not about being better than others. You've woven different strengths into each of us to complement one another in the body of Christ. You're not asking me to imitate anyone else, you're shaping me to look more like Jesus. In Jesus's name, amen.

DAY 36

Rooted Relationships

God made me to be in relationship with others.

And the LORD God said, "*It is* not good that man should be alone; I will make him a helper comparable to him."

—GENESIS 2:18

Dear heavenly Father, you created us for connection not just with you, but with one another. And to be honest, it feels safer to put up walls than risk being hurt. Help me experience your gift of connection to nurture real, safe companionship that is rooted in your love. Protect me from relationships that pull me away from you and open my heart to the people you want in my life. Surround me with a community I can grow with, where I'm known, loved, challenged, and where you're at the center. In Jesus's name, amen.

DAY 37

Heal My Broken Heart

God can heal my trauma.

The LORD *is* near to those who have a broken heart,
And saves such as have a contrite spirit.

Many *are* the afflictions of the righteous,
But the LORD delivers him out of them all.
He guards all his bones;
Not one of them is broken.

—PSALM 34:18-20

Dear Lord, life in this world can be filled with traumatic and painful wounds. I long to experience life in the Garden of Eden before sin brought brokenness into the world. I know I won't see wholeness on this side of heaven, but please heal my wounds and scars. I lay it all before you: events I wish never happened, questions I still don't have answers for, pain I don't understand and no one else sees. In Jesus's name, amen.

DAY 38

Give to God First

Give to God first and he will give freely to you.

Honor the LORD with your possessions,
And with the firstfruits of all your increase . . .

—PROVERBS 3:9

Dear heavenly Father, your word tells me that if I honor you with my firstfruits, I will receive your increase—I will have more than enough and will never go without. I pray that I am always willing to give to you. Teach me to wisely steward the monetary resources you entrust me with. I trust that you will continue to provide in abundance, and free me of a mindset that comes from a place of scarcity. Please guide my decisions to reflect your will over my finances so that I can use them to bless others and bring you glory. In Jesus's name, amen.

DAY 39

The Work of Patience

Perfect patience is found in the Lord.

But let patience have *its* perfect work, that you may be perfect and complete, lacking nothing.

—JAMES 1:4

Dear God, you ask me to be patient because you do your deepest work in the waiting. I have a hard time having patience for myself, others, and ultimately, your timing for my life. Waiting for something to be resolved or to experience a breakthrough can feel like wasted time or that you've forgotten me altogether. Remind me that you aren't just working out the outcome, but you're working in me, to prepare me to become the woman you've created me to be. In Jesus's name, amen.

DAY 40

Freedom from Idols

I pray God tears down my idols.

They served their idols,
Which became a snare to them.

—PSALM 106:36

Dear God, my heart drifts from you when I put my focus and efforts to define my identity, value, or security based on metrics that I establish for myself. I confess and admit that even good things can be idols when they demand more of my time and attention than you, and in these moments, my faith can feel fragile. If there's anything I've put above you in my heart, show me what it is. Tear down every idol and help me worship you alone. In Jesus's name, amen.

DAY 41

Our Heart's Treasures

The Lord has my heart; he is my greatest treasure.

For where your treasure is, there your heart will be also.

—MATTHEW 6:21

Dear heavenly Father, I don't want the distractions of this world to captivate my heart. Wean me off the things that I rely on more than you. I want my heart to be brimming with what is important to you. Focus my heart on what has eternal value. Let your eyes be my eyes and your heart be my heart so I can fully know what it means to walk in faith because you are the true and only treasure I need. In Jesus's name, amen.

DAY 42

United by Perfect Love

Love unites.

But above all these things put on love, which is the bond of perfection.

—COLOSSIANS 3:14

Dear Father God, when I am in disagreement with others, may your perfect love bring me back into unity, not only with each other, but in you and your perfect plan. Soften our hearts to give grace to one another, to create space to step outside of our own experiences and hurts so that we can see one another through your eyes, and generously extend compassion to your precious children. Thank you for your love and your Holy Spirit to unify us. In Jesus's name, amen.

DAY 43

Cherished and Honored

I am precious in the sight of God.

Since you were precious in My sight,
You have been honored,
And I have loved you;
Therefore I will give men for you,
And people for your life.

—ISAIAH 43:4

Dear heavenly Father, you call me precious not because of what I've done, but because I am yours. You formed me, loved me, and covered me in Christ's righteousness. You've removed my sin and shame and clothed me with dignity and strength. In your eyes, I am deeply loved and seated in heavenly places. In all these ways, you've honored me and shown me how precious I am to you. I want to honor you in word, deed, and thought, in Jesus's name, amen.

DAY 44

Seeking Direction

I want to follow the Lord, trusting him in all things.

When they heard the king, they departed; and behold, the star which they had seen in the East went before them, till it came and stood over where the young Child was.

—MATTHEW 2:9

Dear Father, the wise men that came to Bethlehem for Jesus's birth chose to obey the divine order over earthly authority. They trusted your leading and followed a star that gave a direct path to Jesus and rejoiced! I want to follow that same unmistakable course that will lead me directly to you, with the same clarity to know that you are always leading me. In Jesus's name, amen.

DAY 45

In the Wilderness

I find true joy in Christ alone.

And you shall remember that the Lord your God led you all the way these forty years in the wilderness, to humble you *and* test you, to know what *was* in your heart, whether you would keep His commandments or not.

—DEUTERONOMY 8:2

Dear God, I try to find happiness and value in things that never truly satisfy, keeping me stuck in old patterns, but expecting different outcomes. I release those counterfeit sources of identity and worth and choose to let you fill my heart instead. Even when I face temptation and tests, I know that as I endure them you never leave my side. In Jesus's name, amen.

DAY 46

A Daughter of the King

As a daughter of the King, I am a co-heir with Christ.

The Spirit Himself bears witness with our spirit that we are children of God, and if children, then heirs—heirs of God and joint heirs with Christ, if indeed we suffer with *Him*, that we may also be glorified together.

—ROMANS 8:16–17

Dear Lord, thank you for calling me your daughter. On my own, I feel unworthy, but Jesus made me priceless when he died for my sins. You say that I am a joint heir with Christ, and that I belong to you. In moments of isolation or loneliness, let this truth be a balm and provide for me the security I need to keep going. Thank you for adopting me into your family. In Jesus's name, amen.

DAY 47

The Gift of Salvation

I have been saved by God's marvelous grace.

For by grace you have been saved through faith, and that not of yourselves; *it is* the gift of God, not of works, lest anyone should boast.

—EPHESIANS 2:8–9

Dear Father God, I remember the first time I recognized and realized I had faith and felt your presence on my heart. My heart flooded with humility and thanksgiving to understand the debt that was paid when Jesus sacrificed his life for me. I deeply felt the love you freely give. In my everyday life, I confess I forget that intimate encounter although I label myself as a believer. Keep that moment alive as I live out each day, and may I never lose that sense of awe when I think of my salvation. Give me fresh eyes whenever I look to you. In Jesus's name, amen.

DAY 48

A Heart of Submission

I want to submit to God in all things.

Then Mary said, "Behold the maidservant of the Lord! Let it be to me according to your word." And the angel departed from her.

—LUKE 1:38

Dear Father, when the angel appeared before Mary and declared that she would give birth to the Son of God, she was uncertain, and troubled to be singled out, as the Lord had highly favored her. But as your plan revealed, Mary's heart opens to be your servant, ready for total surrender to do your will—fulfilling a crucial role that led to Jesus as our Savior. Like Mary, I wonder why you chose me to fulfill a purpose or calling whether it's through certain circumstances, positions of privilege, or roles. I am meek and unqualified to meet his perfection and your plan might not be clear right away in the immediate future or for even in this lifetime to me, but I pray that you will give me her same heart! In Jesus's name I pray, amen.

DAY 49

Encouragement Is Abundant

Hope, joy, and peace are found in Christ.

Now may the God of hope fill you with all joy and peace in believing, that you may abound in hope by the power of the Holy Spirit.

—ROMANS 15:13

Dear Lord, thank you that true hope, joy, and peace are found in you. In any circumstance, I want to come to you to experience encouragement. When the enemy comes to steal my joy, your Holy Spirit reminds me that I have an endless supply of joy because I am tethered to you. In Jesus's name, amen.

DAY 50

In Spirit and In Truth

I worship the Lord with all that I am.

"'These people draw near to Me with their mouth,
And honor Me with *their* lips,
But their heart is far from Me.
And in vain they worship Me,
Teaching as doctrines the commandments of men.'"

—MATTHEW 15:8–9

Dear heavenly Father, I want to worship you with an undivided and surrendered heart that seeks to be near you. Delight in my praise and make my worship less about what I can gain and more about you. It's easy to mistake worship for chasing an emotional high, but let my love and awe of you be at the center of my praise. In Jesus's name, amen.

DAY 51

Seasons and Rhythms of Grace

There is a time for everything.

To everything *there is* a season,
A time for every purpose under heaven . . .

—ECCLESIASTES 3:1

Dear Lord, your timing is perfect. You command the rising and setting of the sun, and the budding and falling of leaves. Every season carries its own purpose that you've designed. Thank you for the season I'm in so I can move in step with your rhythm for my life. When I'm in a season of hardship, I know a season of rejoicing is just around the corner. Remind me that I can trust in your perfect time frame, not my own. In Jesus's name, amen.

DAY 52

Slow to Anger

Make me slow to anger.

He who is slow to anger *is* better than the mighty,
And he who rules his spirit than he who takes a city.

—PROVERBS 16:32

Dear heavenly Father, my anger is usually a mask for what lies underneath the surface, whether it's hurt, fear, frustration, shame, or grief. When I feel anger, help me pause, and reflect, so you can reveal the true source of my pain. Teach me to bring what I'm feeling to you; instead of lashing out, give me courage to examine deeper within me to find what's bubbling up as anger. In Jesus's name, amen.

DAY 53

Walk Like Christ

I want to be like Christ.

Therefore be merciful, just as your Father also is merciful.

—LUKE 6:36

But when the kindness and the love of God our Savior toward man appeared, not by works of righteousness which we have done, but according to His mercy He saved us, through the washing of regeneration and renewing of the Holy Spirit, whom He poured out on us abundantly through Jesus Christ our Savior . . .

—TITUS 3:4-6

Dear God, you extended forgiveness and pardoned our sins through Jesus's sacrifice on the cross, and his death was the ultimate expression of your mercy. He sat with the rejected, he gave his heart to the suffering and the brokenhearted, and healed the sick. Light in me the same compassion that Jesus led with: to generously extend your love to people around me and to glorify you with all that I do, because I experienced his mercy firsthand. Thank you for the gift of Jesus. In Jesus's name, amen.

DAY 54

Walk in Truth

We always get caught in our snares.

A false witness will not go unpunished,
And *he who* speaks lies will not escape.

—PROVERBS 19:5

Dear God, you see all things and nothing is hidden from you! You see me when I bend the truth, whether it's to protect myself or others in ways that are seemingly harmless. But you show me that when I stretch the truth, to make myself appear better, it comes at a cost—it erodes trust and diminishes my relationships. Help me to be truthful, in all things, big and small. Give me a transparent heart that delights in the truth because you're a God who treasures it. In Jesus's name, amen.

DAY 55

Peace that Surpasses Understanding

I want the peace of God all the time.

And the peace of God, which surpasses all understanding, will guard your hearts and minds through Christ Jesus.

—PHILIPPIANS 4:7

Dear God, you promise a peace that keeps my heart and mind safe. When I center my focus on you, you give me a calm that isn't tied to perfect circumstances but to the presence of a perfect God. Let my heart and mind overflow with your perfect peace. Keep me from being thrown off course by anything that distracts me from centering on you. In Jesus's name, amen.

DAY 56

Delight in the Lord

If I delight in God, he will give me the desires of my heart.

Delight yourself also in the LORD,
And He shall give you the desires of your heart.

—PSALM 37:4

Dear Lord, thank you for filling my heart with your desires when I delight in you. You know what is best for me! I want to follow your way, not what I think is right in my own eyes. I don't want to focus on my desires for what is fleeting in this life, I just want to focus on you because you are my God yesterday, today, and forever. In Jesus's name, amen.

DAY 57

Building Others Up in Love

We are all always learning and growing.

Let each of us please *his* neighbor for *his* good, leading to edification.

—ROMANS 15:2

Dear God, work in me to love as Jesus instructs us. Please give me the ability to reach others in a way that speaks to them personally, whether it's through acts of service, words, gifts, quality time, or physical affection to feel loved. Use the way I love others as a way to share how deeply and personally you care for us and how we each need and want to be loved. In Jesus's name, amen.

DAY 58

Matchless Grace

We can never fall too far from God's grace.

Then he said to Jesus, "Lord, remember me when You come into Your kingdom."
And Jesus said to him, "Assuredly, I say to you, today you will be with Me in Paradise."

—LUKE 23:42-43

Dear Jesus, you saved a dying thief on the cross because he simply turned to you and believed the words that were meant for him. He had nothing to offer you, no time to clean himself up. Even in what would've appeared to be your most powerless moment, you were willing to save anyone who came to you, no matter what they did or how late they come to you. Help me remember that no one is ever too far gone for your grace, even me. Give me the eyes to see others through the same grace. In your beautiful name, amen.

DAY 59

Empowered by His Spirit

I can lean on Jesus when things don't go as I plan.

"Most assuredly, I say to you, he who believes in Me, the works that I do he will do also; and greater *works* than these he will do, because I go to My Father. And whatever you ask in My name, that I will do, that the Father may be glorified in the Son."

—JOHN 14:12–13

Dear heavenly Father, I tend to approach each day with a mission to accomplish what I set out to do. And more days than not, things rarely go exactly as planned or as I expect. Sometimes, it even goes in devastating ways—a loss of a loved one, a health setback, an emergency that I cannot step in to fix, or when an opportunity falls through. And in these moments, I want to still feel empowered because you promise that you are strength. When my spirit is dimmed, please open my eyes to see that your vision is far better than what I fixate on in my present state. Soothe and reassure me that you will uplift this heavy heart. In Jesus's name I pray, amen.

DAY 60

So Loved

I am so cherished by God that he gave his one and only Son up for me.

For God so loved the world that He gave His only begotten Son, that whoever believes in Him should not perish but have everlasting life.

—JOHN 3:16

Dear Jesus, you died not for your benefit, but for mine. You took my place, taking on the weight of sin so I could be free. You didn't wait for me to be good enough—you love me at my worst. You suffered unimaginably, in every way, so I could have eternal life with you. I'll never fully grasp that kind of love, but I thank you for loving me so much. Shape my heart to respond to your love in all I do. In your name, amen.

DAY 61

I Am Precious

I am precious in God's sight.

"Are not five sparrows sold for two copper coins? And not one of them is forgotten before God. But the very hairs of your head are all numbered. Do not fear therefore; you are of more value than many sparrows."

—LUKE 12:6-7

Dear Jesus, how encouraging it is to know that God values each creation and is beloved by you. I am precious in your eyes. When I'm discouraged by the world, feeling depleted, insecure in my efforts, or feeling lesser than my peers, you say I matter, you say I am loved, you say I have purpose. This gives me courage to live out each day with meaning. Thank you and in your name I pray, amen.

DAY 62

Faithful Friends

I was made for friendship.

Then behold, men brought on a bed a man who was paralyzed, whom they sought to bring in and lay before Him. And when they could not find how they might bring him in, because of the crowd, they went up on the housetop and let him down with *his* bed through the tiling into the midst before Jesus. When He saw their faith, He said to him, "Man, your sins are forgiven you."

—LUKE 5:18-20

Dear Jesus, I want to be the friend that will climb rooftops if that's what it takes to save them. Grant me a strong faith like the men who lowered the paraplegic man through the roof, whose belief in you moved you to heal. Hear my prayer for the healing of those I love. I lift them up to you to give them the comfort they need when they feel alone and isolated in their pain. In your precious name, amen.

DAY 63

Confessing Is Belief

When I confess, he is shaping me.

But what does it say? "The word is near you, in your mouth and in your heart" (that is, the word of faith which we preach): that if you confess with your mouth the Lord Jesus and believe in your heart that God has raised Him from the dead, you will be saved.

—ROMANS 10:8-9

Dear heavenly Father, you see my every thought, action, emotion, hope, and need. Give me the confidence to live out each day like I truly believe it and truly believe you are next to me. Even though you witness each of my thoughts, you want to hear my confession. I want to release my shame because you embrace me and I confess because Jesus bravely died for my personal sins. I am thankful that you are a God who is for us. In Jesus's name, amen.

DAY 64

Direct My Steps

Even when I'm overwhelmed, God holds my future.

The steps of a *good* man are ordered by the LORD,
And He delights in his way.

—PSALM 37:23

Dear Lord, when David was overwhelmed and everyone was out to get him, he turned to you for direction. Just as you guided King David, when I face overwhelming moments in my life, when I'm drowning in my to-do list, swirling in emotions, or facing disappointment from unmet expectations, help me trust that you're directing my every step forward, even when I can't clearly see what the path looks like ahead. In Jesus's name, amen.

DAY 65

Out of the Boat

I always step toward God.

But immediately Jesus spoke to them, saying, "Be of good cheer! It is I; do not be afraid."
And Peter answered Him and said, "Lord, if it is You, command me to come to You on the water."
So He said, "Come." And when Peter had come down out of the boat, he walked on the water to go to Jesus. But when he saw that the wind *was* boisterous, he was afraid; and beginning to sink he cried out, saying, "Lord, save me!"

—MATTHEW 14:27–30

Dear Jesus, no matter what storm I'm in, even when everything feels completely out of control, you empower me to step toward you. Just like you called Peter to step out of the boat, you invite me to step out of what feels safe and what keeps me stuck. True freedom begins when I trust you more than my desire to stay comfortable. Help me venture out in faith, to leave what's familiar and to follow you. In your name, amen.

DAY 66

By His Strength

When I am at the end of myself, that's where God's strength comes in.

Not that we are sufficient of ourselves to think of anything as *being* from ourselves, but our sufficiency *is* from God . . .

—2 CORINTHIANS 3:5

Dear God, I am exhausted. Life seems to demand from me until I don't have much left to give. When I try to run on my own strength, willpower, and effort, I feel so limited. Keep my eyes on you so I may have a steady source of strength from you. You are the strength I need daily. In Jesus's name, amen.

DAY 67

Everlasting Throne

God is on the throne, from everlasting to everlasting.

Before the mountains were brought forth, Or ever You had formed the earth and the world, Even from everlasting to everlasting, You *are* God.

—PSALM 90:2

Dear heavenly Father, you existed before the world began and you will exist long after, outside of space and time. I am thankful I serve a God who so rules over the heavens and the earth and yet, you mercifully care about me and walk with me on my journey. Thank you, Lord, for your love. In Jesus's name, amen.

DAY 68

Holy Spirit and Vision

Give me eyes to see what you have for me, Lord.

"And it shall come to pass afterward
That I will pour out My Spirit on all flesh;
Your sons and your daughters shall prophesy,
Your old men shall dream dreams,
Your young men shall see visions."

—JOEL 2:28

Dear heavenly Father, your Holy Spirit lives in me and guides me in all things. I pray that I can clearly see the plans you've placed in my heart for me to do, that you answer and confirm what you have planned for me. Please reveal your answers in prayer and in your word. In Jesus's name, amen.

DAY 69

Becoming Better Not Bitter

Everything but God will leave me empty.

But she said to them, "Do not call me Naomi; call me Mara, for the Almighty has dealt very bitterly with me. I went out full, and the LORD has brought me home again empty. Why do you call me Naomi, since the LORD has testified against me, and the Almighty has afflicted me?"

—RUTH 1:20–21

Dear God, loss of loved ones or stability leaves me feeling disappointed and discouraged. Naomi's bitterness is so relatable in the face of grief; I'm tempted to believe that you've forgotten about me. Help me to hold on to the truth: You truly see what is under my bitterness. When things feel unfair and hopeless, please show me a way forward to release and heal my wound. You still are near me, even when I feel unworthy of love. You lighten my load, your love restores and redeems me. In Jesus's name, amen.

DAY 70

Walk in Wisdom

God gives wisdom freely.

For the LORD gives wisdom;
From His mouth *come* knowledge and understanding;
He stores up sound wisdom for the upright;
He is a shield to those who walk uprightly . . .

—PROVERBS 2:6-7

Dear Father God, when I don't know what to do, I want to turn to you for guidance—you are the source of all wisdom and hope. Let me grow in wisdom day by day—not just in what I understand intellectually, but how I live. When I need your instruction, I want to hear from you clearly so there is no mistake or hesitation in knowing how you want me to move forward. Thank you for always giving me the prudence and insight I need. In Jesus's name, amen.

DAY 71

Perseverance in Trials

I can persevere even through trials.

And not only *that,* but we also glory in tribulations, knowing that tribulation produces perseverance; and perseverance, character; and character, hope.

—ROMANS 5:3-4

Dear Lord, you use trials as instruments to grow my faith and ask patience and efforts of me to shape me into the likeness of Jesus. Walking with you isn't easy, but I thank you for the challenges that have drawn me closer to you. Give me the endurance to move through difficult times. Remind me that pain is not in vain, that you're always with me to overcome any trial I'm up against. In Jesus's name, amen.

DAY 72
Weariness

When I am weak in spirit, the Lord will give me strength.

"What man of you, having a hundred sheep, if he loses one of them, does not leave the ninety-nine in the wilderness, and go after the one which is lost until he finds it? And when he has found *it*, he lays *it* on his shoulders, rejoicing."

—LUKE 15:4-5

Dear God, thank you for providing me with your strength when I have none left. When I am depleted to keep going, it comforts me to know that you will still find me and carry me to rest. When I am astray, you lead me in the ways I need to go. You came in human form and experienced suffering, weakness, temptation. You understand and know exactly what I am going through. I was lost and now I am found. In Jesus's name, amen.

DAY 73
Called and Chosen

I was called, but I was also chosen.

"For many are called, but few *are* chosen."

—MATTHEW 22:14

Dear Lord, you've extended an invitation to everyone, but only a few accept. Thank you for choosing me to be part of your story. Help me share that invitation with others, not just in words but through a love that reflects Jesus—especially to those the world tends to overlook. Let my life point others to the privilege and joy of being chosen. In Jesus's name, amen.

DAY 74

What Matters Most

Outward beauty is fleeting, but inward beauty is forever.

Do not let your adornment be *merely* outward—arranging the hair, wearing gold, or putting on *fine* apparel—rather *let it be* the hidden person of the heart, with the incorruptible *beauty* of a gentle and quiet spirit, which is very precious in the sight of God.

—1 PETER 3:3-4

But the LORD said to Samuel, "Do not look at his appearance or at his physical stature, because I have refused him. For *the* LORD *does* not *see* as man sees; for man looks at the outward appearance, but the LORD looks at the heart."

—1 SAMUEL 16:7

Dear Lord, I look at others around me and notice where I don't measure up, whether it's through looks, talents, accomplishments, or confidence. Remind me that what you care more about isn't on the surface, but the state of my heart. Outward circumstances always change and fade, but the inward beauty of a gentle and kind spirit is precious in your sight. Center me to build my character, cultivate my humility, compassion, and a quiet strength. In Jesus's name, amen.

DAY 75

No Room for Shame

There is no place for shame in God's love.

For the Scripture says, "Whoever believes on Him will not be put to shame."

—ROMANS 10:11

Dear God, you have redeemed me. I bring every part of me that is broken by shame into the light of your compassion and truth. Help me see myself the way you see me and who you call me to be, not through lies that say I'm unworthy or unloved. Remind me that what Jesus did on the cross is greater than any shame I feel. In Jesus's name, amen.

DAY 76

Uprooting Bitterness

Breathe life to joy, weed out all bitterness.

Let all bitterness, wrath, anger, clamor, and evil speaking be put away from you, with all malice.

—EPHESIANS 4:31

Pursue peace with all *people*, and holiness, without which no one will see the Lord: looking carefully lest anyone fall short of the grace of God; lest any root of bitterness springing up cause trouble, and by this many become defiled . . .

—HEBREWS 12:14-15

Dear Lord, bitterness can sneak into my heart and chain me to old wounds from my past. The danger of becoming bitter is that it distorts how I see others and steals my peace. Holy Spirit, weed out the sharpness in my heart before it takes root and spreads. Prune my heart, and let forgiveness and joy grow in its place. In Jesus's name, amen.

DAY 77

Forgiveness Is Essential

Help me to forgive freely.

"And whenever you stand praying, if you have anything against anyone, forgive him, that your Father in heaven may also forgive you your trespasses."

—MARK 11:25

Dear heavenly Father, I'm struggling to forgive myself today. I repeat past offenses and mistakes in my mind, and the regret keeps me from caring for my heart in a way that is honoring to you. I want to release these obstacles and be closer to you. Please speak into my heart so I can forgive freely, not just to myself but to others, just as you did. When I don't know where to start, remind me I can start with "Our Father who art in heaven . . ." In Jesus's name I pray, amen.

DAY 78

Freedom in Truth

He is Liberty.

Now the Lord is the Spirit; and where the Spirit of the Lord *is*, there *is* liberty.

—2 CORINTHIANS 3:17

Dear Lord, you are the way, the truth, and the life (John 14:6). Transform my heart so I am a willing follower as your faithful witness. Since true freedom is found in a relationship with Jesus, help me to resist the temptations of relying on myself and instead remain faithful and obedient to you, the giver of all good things. In Jesus's name, amen.

DAY 79

Glory to God Alone

Pride comes before the fall.

Pride goes before destruction,
And a haughty spirit before a fall.

—PROVERBS 16:18

Dear God, pride sneaks its way undetected and grows when I am preoccupied with myself. Lucifer pursued his own recognition and turned his ministry of worshipping you into a stage for applause. And we are inundated with a similar message today: that happiness is found in the worship of self instead of God. Guard my mind from these prideful, self-congratulatory, and self-righteous beliefs because there is no higher honor than praising you. In Jesus's name, amen.

DAY 80

A Prepared Table

Help me to focus on the harvest, not the challenges.

You prepare a table before me in the presence of my enemies;
You anoint my head with oil;
My cup runs over.

—PSALM 23:5

Dear heavenly Father, I'm sorry for the times I dwell on those who've hurt me or chase after things that pull me away from you. Yet in the middle of it all, you still offer a seat next to you. Thank you for welcoming me to your table, not because I have it all together, but because you are full of grace. Help me to see the victory and blessings you've already placed in front of me. My cup truly overflows. In Jesus's name, amen.

DAY 81

Asking for Answers

When I ask, God opens the door.

"Ask, and it will be given to you; seek, and you will find; knock, and it will be opened to you. For everyone who asks receives, and he who seeks finds, and to him who knocks it will be opened."

—MATTHEW 7:7-8

Dear Lord Jesus, in times of transition, change, or opportunity, thank you for granting me this season of life. If it comes under less than ideal circumstances or in plentiful abundance, or I face a decision without knowing the outcome, you teach us to ask, seek, and knock, and you will answer. I pray for wise judgment and even if the answer might be obvious, slow my heart to hear your voice in each step along the way so that I may truly follow your answer. In your name, amen.

DAY 82

The Beauty of Your Presence

He is good.

Enter into His gates with thanksgiving,
And into His courts with praise.
Be thankful to Him, *and* bless His name.
For the LORD *is* good;
His mercy *is* everlasting,
And His truth *endures* to all generations.

—PSALM 100:4-5

Dear Lord, when I enter into your presence, you pull me out of the darkness and into your marvelous light, where you always welcome me with open arms. Your presence opens my eyes to the truth that you are a God who sees every part of me and loves me wholly and unconditionally. My heart is filled with gratitude because of your goodness and everlasting mercy. In Jesus's name, amen.

DAY 83

Giver of All Gifts

Guard my heart from the love of money.

He who loves silver will not be satisfied with silver;
Nor he who loves abundance, with increase.
This also *is* vanity.

—ECCLESIASTES 5:10

And He said to them, "Take heed and beware of covetousness, for one's life does not consist in the abundance of the things he possesses."

—LUKE 12:15

Dear Father God, thank you for entrusting me with the gift of life! Teach me to steward what you've given me with wisdom, generosity, and an eternal purpose. I pray that I cherish today and each day to express my gratitude and receive your blessings. In Jesus's name, amen.

DAY 84

Created by You and for You

I was created by God and for God.

For by Him all things were created that are in heaven and that are on earth, visible and invisible, whether thrones or dominions or principalities or powers. All things were created through Him and for Him.

—COLOSSIANS 1:16

Dear Lord, it's no accident that I'm here. The God who created the moon, sun, and stars also created me. I'm imperfect and unworthy of your glory, and yet, I'm your treasured possession. I was created for a Creator—the One who knows me better than anyone. Thank you for calling me yours. In Jesus's name, amen.

DAY 85

Eternal Life

This life is temporary, but God is forever.

For we know that if our earthly house, *this* tent, is destroyed, we have a building from God, a house not made with hands, eternal in the heavens.

—2 CORINTHIANS 5:1

Dear heavenly Father, everything on this earth is temporary but you are eternal. Our time on earth is a shelter, a resting place, but you say our true home is in heaven with you. You designed a place for me and eagerly wait for me to enjoy it. Thank you, Jesus, for the guarantee of my inheritance in eternal life. In Jesus's name I pray, amen.

DAY 86

Miraculous Healing

I want to see miracles of healing in my midst.

Confess *your* trespasses to one another, and pray for one another, that you may be healed. The effective, fervent prayer of a righteous man avails much.

—JAMES 5:16

Dear Jesus, you are the Great Physician and miracle worker. You brought healing to the sick, sight to the blind, strength to the weak, and life to the dead. But you didn't just come to heal physical wounds, you came to free us from the weight of sin, not just in the past or future, but now, today, for me. I thank you for being by my side. In your name, amen.

DAY 87

No Going Back

The Lord helps me to resist all sin.

Therefore if the Son makes you free, you shall be free indeed.

—JOHN 8:36

For you, brethren, have been called to liberty; only do not *use* liberty as an opportunity for the flesh, but through love serve one another.

—GALATIANS 5:13

Dear Jesus, you didn't save me from the bondage of sin so I could live a comfortable life. You saved me so I could be free to serve others and walk in love. Your freedom gives me the power to resist what holds me captive. Help me use my freedom to love and serve others, not to live for myself. In your loving name, amen.

DAY 88

GOD'S TIMING

He always answers in his perfect timing.

Now Martha said to Jesus, "Lord, if You had been here, my brother would not have died. But even now I know that whatever You ask of God, God will give You."
Jesus said to her, "Your brother will rise again."

—JOHN 11:21–23

Jesus said to her, "Did I not say to you that if you would believe you would see the glory of God?"

—JOHN 11:40

Dear Jesus, when I don't get an answer to prayer right away, whether I'm asking for healing or clarity, I am discouraged when nothing seems to change. Remind me that you see the whole picture and you're never too late. A situation might seem to be getting worse, but when you intervene, you reveal your power in a way that glorifies the Father. Even when Martha may have felt disappointment that her brother had died before you arrived to heal him, she still trusted you. Sometimes I misunderstand what you're doing, but you demonstrate that even in loss, there is hope. In my grief, I can still expect you. In your almighty name, amen.

DAY 89

Made Well

Being open to healing.

When Jesus saw him lying there, and knew that he already had been *in that condition* a long time, He said to him, "Do you want to be made well?"

—JOHN 5:6

Dear heavenly Father, I can get so focused on my pain, what's been done to me, what I've lost, or fixate on why things haven't changed, that I end up holding on to the hurt tighter than I am to you. Give me grace for these areas that still need your healing. If any part of me has grown comfortable with staying where I am, stir in me a desire to be made whole. I want to lay aside any excuse I've clung to and be open to your healing. In Jesus's name, amen.

DAY 90

God Is Healing My Past

The hope I have in the Lord is powerful.

When You said, "Seek My face,"
My heart said to You, "Your face, LORD, I will seek."

PSALM 27:8

Dear heavenly Father, my past sometimes still affects me in ways I don't expect. Thoughts crop up and trigger my emotions, and my heart feels tender. Through these moments, I know you're inviting me to seek your face, to experience more of your presence. Walk with me through them, heal what still hurts, and fill me with your peace and hope. My hope is in you, and the future you have for me is greater than any trigger from my past. Restore and renew me. In Jesus's name, amen.

DAY 91

Second Chances

We serve a God of second chances, even when we run in the opposite direction.

Who *is* a God like You,
Pardoning iniquity
And passing over the transgression of the remnant of His heritage?
He does not retain His anger forever,
Because He delights *in* mercy.

—MICAH 7:18

Dear heavenly Father, when I fall short or avoid you, you call me to return even when I choose my way time and time again. Even when Jonah went against your will and fled from what you were calling him to do, you still used him to save the people of Nineveh. Sometimes I feel so unworthy to be used by you, but you're a loving God of second chances. In Jesus's name, amen.

DAY 92

Renew My Strength

God renews my strength, even when I'm overwhelmed.

He gives power to the weak,
And to *those who have* no might He increases strength.

—ISAIAH 40:29

Dear Father God, when the weight of my burdens feels unbearable, and I'm overwhelmed from trying to carry it all on my own, you give me the rest I need. Help me see that it's not up to me to fix everything and that I can place it all in your hands. Remind me that I can constantly give you my burdens. I want to rest in your presence, knowing you continually renew my strength. In Jesus's name, amen.

DAY 93

Help Me Believe

Belief equals breakthrough.

Immediately the father of the child cried out and said with tears, "Lord, I believe; help my unbelief!"

—MARK 9:24

Dear Abba Father, when I struggle with doubt or apathy, bring me to your word when my heart is unwilling to soften. When I seem to overlook your presence, bring me to spend time in the Word so I can remember all your miraculous works and meet you, waiting for me. You are there in my moments of doubt and unbelief. By your grace, my faith can grow deeper day by day because I can turn to you and your word to remember that I have the anchor I need to walk victoriously in Christ. In Jesus's name, amen.

DAY 94

Faith Over Fear

I do not need to fear; I can trust God through it all.

In God (I will praise His word),
In God I have put my trust;
I will not fear.
What can flesh do to me?

—PSALM 56:4

Dear heavenly Father, you've shown me that faith doesn't mean I won't feel fear, it means I trust you through it. In Gethsemane, Jesus wrestled the weight of the cross, yet surrendered fully. Like Noah, who obeyed despite the ridicule and dry skies, help me walk in faith even when I don't see the outcome. When fear creeps in, you are near, steady, and trustworthy. In Jesus's name, amen.

DAY 95

Searching for Precious Worth

I recognize the infinite value of Jesus.

"Again, the kingdom of heaven is like a merchant seeking beautiful pearls, who, when he had found one pearl of great price, went and sold all that he had and bought it."

—MATTHEW 13:45–46

Dear heavenly Father, Jesus shares the parable of a merchant searching for beautiful pearls who uproots his whole life when he discovers a precious one. I can be like the merchant, searching for meaning and purpose for my life in all the wrong places, even when your pursuit of me is in plain sight. Course correct my heart so I can transform my ways to follow you in the same way Jesus pursues us as his precious pearl, sacrificing everything to redeem us. In Jesus's name, amen.

DAY 96

Finding Hidden Treasure

The Lord is my treasure.

"Again, the kingdom of heaven is like treasure hidden in a field, which a man found and hid; and for joy over it he goes and sells all that he has and buys that field."

—MATTHEW 13:44

Dear Father God, to believe in and know you is a treasure beyond all measure. Thank you for the gift of salvation I could never earn, and you've allowed me to freely choose. You invite us to ask and receive, to seek and find, to knock and the door will open (Matthew 7:7–8). When we pursue you, you always reveal yourself to us. Help others to search and find the treasure of salvation. In Jesus's name, amen.

DAY 97

Master Builder

Have confidence in the Lord while waiting.

Being confident of this very thing, that He who has begun a good work in you will complete *it* until the day of Jesus Christ . . .

—PHILIPPIANS 1:6

Dear Father God, you're a master builder. You sketched my blueprint, poured the foundation, and have never left a project incomplete. I sometimes doubt your plan when I see your unfinished work. I wonder how anything beautiful could come of today's mess. Help me not to focus on a single granular moment but remember this is just one piece of the masterpiece you're creating. When you finally unveil your finished work, I'll stand in awe of how everything unfolds and every piece of my life fit together. In Jesus's name, amen.

DAY 98

Stewarding God's Gifts

Give and you will receive.

So Jesus answered and said, "Assuredly, I say to you, there is no one who has left house or brothers or sisters or father or mother or wife or children or lands, for My sake and the gospel's, who shall not receive a hundredfold now in this time—houses and brothers and sisters and mothers and children and lands, with persecutions—and in the age to come, eternal life . . ."

—MARK 10:29–30

Dear Lord, your word promises that when I give, I'll receive abundance. Give me a heart that reflects your love and generosity because everything I have is a gift from you. I give thanks for all you offer me, both in this earthly life and in eternity. When I get stuck in a mindset of scarcity and survival, help me remember that you enrich my days with everything I need. Let me truly feel and know this truth deeply. Thank you for sustaining me. Show me how to steward what you give me with wisdom. In Jesus's name, amen.

DAY 99

FREEDOM FROM MUSTS AND OUGHTS

I *get to* spend time with the Lord, not *I have to.*

My voice You shall hear in the morning, O LORD;
In the morning I will direct *it* to You,
And I will look up.

—PSALM 5:3

Dear God, when going to church, praying, and reading the Bible start becoming things I have to do rather than things I want to do, it's because I've started to forget the joy of being motivated by your love for me, not an obligatory list of rules and regulations to be a "good" Christian. Free me from ideas about earning your love through my efforts or whether I'm doing enough. I take rest by staying connected in your love, not in tirelessly doing more. In Jesus's name, amen.

DAY 100

THE POWER OF GOD LIVES IN ME

The same power that lived in Jesus now lives in me.

Yes, we had the sentence of death in ourselves, that we should not trust in ourselves but in God who raises the dead, who delivered us from so great a death, and does deliver us; in whom we trust that He will still deliver us . . .

—2 CORINTHIANS 1:9–10

Dear God, there are days I wonder if I'll ever fully overcome my struggles—whether it's how I navigate relationships, old habits, engage in negative self-talk, or my pride. You give me victory through Christ, even when I don't feel it. The same power that raised Jesus and brought Lazarus back to life now lives in me through the Holy Spirit. Turn my heart to you when I'm tempted to slip back into old ways—you're always at work in me. In Jesus's name, amen.

DAY 101

Identity in Christ

I am a new creation in Christ.

I have been crucified with Christ; it is no longer I who live, but Christ lives in me; and the *life* which I now live in the flesh I live by faith in the Son of God, who loved me and gave Himself for me.

—GALATIANS 2:20

Dear Lord, thank you for making me a new creation in Christ Jesus. Thank you for my brand-new identity—one that isn't defined by my past or what others think of me, but who I am as your daughter. My old self and old life are dead and gone, and now your Spirit lives in me. Lead the way I speak, act, and the choices I make—to honor you, just like Jesus did while he was here on earth. In Jesus's name, amen.

DAY 102

Made for More

I am made for more because God chose me.

So he said to Him, "O my Lord, how can I save Israel? Indeed my clan *is* the weakest in Manasseh, and I *am* the least in my father's house."
And the LORD said to him, "Surely I will be with you, and you shall defeat the Midianites as one man."

—JUDGES 6:15-16

Dear heavenly Father, you choose the ordinary to do the extraordinary. You used Gideon, even though he was from the weakest clan and lowest in his household, to lead an army. Help me to not shy away from what you've called me to do, because you made me for more than what I imagine. You choose humble servants like Gideon and call them "Mighty Warrior" as a reminder that it's not my strength or abilities, but your power that accomplishes great things. Fulfill your purposes in my life. In Jesus's name, amen.

DAY 103

Boasting in My Weakness

God's grace is enough.

When Jesus heard *it*, He said to them, "Those who are well have no need of a physician, but those who are sick. I did not come to call *the* righteous, but sinners, to repentance."

—MARK 2:17

Dear Jesus, when I reach the end of my strength, you meet me where I am. I try to fix my weaknesses on my own, but your power to transform me is beyond anything I can do alone. As the Great Physician, you tend to those who need you and invite us into a loving relationship with you. When I bring my weaknesses to you, you can work actively in my life. Humble me so I can lay it all down in front of you. In your name, amen.

DAY 104

Made New

I am growing in holiness.

But now having been set free from sin, and having become slaves of God, you have your fruit to holiness, and the end, everlasting life.

—ROMANS 6:22

"And no one puts new wine into old wineskins; or else the new wine bursts the wineskins, the wine is spilled, and the wineskins are ruined. But new wine must be put into new wineskins."

—MARK 2:22

Dear Lord, I thank you for Jesus who set me free from sin. Because of your sacrifice, I am no longer defined by my past, but with the new life you've given me. You didn't just patch me up to put on old wineskins, but you called me to step into a new identity, a new heart, a new way of life and purpose. I can tackle each new day refreshed and free because Jesus is by my side and I am full of hope. In Jesus's name, amen.

DAY 105

God Never Changes

My circumstances change, but God does not.

"For I *am* the Lord, I do not change;
Therefore you are not consumed, O sons of Jacob."

—MALACHI 3:6

Dear heavenly Father, change can be so unsettling. Regardless of my situation, you are the same yesterday, today, and forever (Hebrews 13:8). Teach me to rest in your unchanging nature and hold loosely to what is temporary. When everything around me feels shaky, remind me that you work out every detail together for my good. In Jesus's name, amen.

DAY 106

Unspeakable Joy

Abiding in Christ brings joy.

"As the Father loved Me, I also have loved you; abide in My love. If you keep My commandments, you will abide in My love, just as I have kept My Father's commandments and abide in His love.
"These things I have spoken to you, that My joy may remain in you, and *that* your joy may be full."

—JOHN 15:9-11

Dear God, remaining in you brings me joy. Please diminish my appetite for anything that comes between my faith and keep me connected to you through prayer and your word. As I stay connected in your love, fill me with a radiant joy that is visible to others—a joy that can only be found in Christ. In Jesus's name, amen.

DAY 107

Help My Unbelief

Jesus can show you evidence of his scars.

Then He said to Thomas, "Reach your finger here, and look at My hands; and reach your hand *here*, and put *it* into My side. Do not be unbelieving, but believing." And Thomas answered and said to Him, "My Lord and my God!"

—JOHN 20:27–28

Dear Father God, when Thomas didn't believe that Jesus had risen from the dead, he was not shamed or rebuked for wanting evidence. Jesus personally sought him out, showed his hands, and told him to stop doubting and to believe. I confess that I can struggle with my faith, trusting that Jesus died for me personally. Remind me that when I struggle with this truth, it is an invitation to seek deeper connection with you. I pray that in my wrestling you draw me closer. Help my unbelief (Mark 9:24). In Jesus's name, amen.

DAY 108

Rich in Blessings

Blessings aren't always material.

The blessing of the LORD makes *one* rich,
And He adds no sorrow with it.

—PROVERBS 10:22

Dear Lord, your blessings come in the form of relationships, friendships, abundance, and opportunities. May I always treasure these gifts from you. Assure my heart to remember that wealth is more than what I can quantify with my eyes—my life is made bountiful and rich because I have you. In Jesus's name, amen.

DAY 109

Daily Surrender

I surrender all to Jesus daily.

Then Jesus said to His disciples, "If anyone desires to come after Me, let him deny himself, and take up his cross, and follow Me. For whoever desires to save his life will lose it, but whoever loses his life for My sake will find it. For what profit is it to a man if he gains the whole world, and loses his own soul? Or what will a man give in exchange for his soul?"

—MATTHEW 16:24-26

Dear Father God, please show me where in my life I'm holding too tightly to my comfort and control. Help me fight against the natural inclination to chase recognition and whatever the world calls success. Empower me daily to surrender my will and live fully for you. In Jesus's precious name, amen.

DAY 110

Help Me Forgive

I want to forgive like Jesus did.

Then Jesus said, "Father, forgive them, for they do not know what they do." And they divided His garments and cast lots.

—LUKE 23:34

Dear Jesus, you call me to forgive others, not to excuse the pain they caused me, but because holding on to it is weighing me down. If there's any unforgiveness buried deep inside of me, even if I thought I already dealt with it, reveal it to me so bitterness doesn't blind me to the freedom you offer. I lay it down before you. In your name, amen.

DAY 111

Bear Fruit in Humility

I am uniquely gifted to bear good fruit for the Lord.

By this My Father is glorified, that you bear much fruit; so you will be My disciples.

—JOHN 15:8

Dear Lord, you've gifted each one of your children with unique skills, talents, and strengths. You bless us to discover and apply them in ways that embrace and steward them well, to be a nurturer, lead teams, bridge viewpoints, provide hospitality, whatever form it may be. Please help me discover all the gifts you've placed in me, and please plant my ambitions and aspirations in humility so they may serve your will over my own greed and vision. In Jesus's name, amen.

DAY 112

Saved by Grace

I have been saved by grace through faith.

Who has saved us and called *us* with a holy calling, not according to our works, but according to His own purpose and grace which was given to us in Christ Jesus before time began, but has now been revealed by the appearing of our Savior Jesus Christ, *who* has abolished death and brought life and immortality to light through the gospel . . .

—2 TIMOTHY 1:9-10

Dear heavenly Father, if it wasn't for your marvelous grace, I couldn't be saved. My standing in Christ is because as Jesus said on the cross when he paid for every sin, "It is finished." When I try to strive to prove myself or be good enough, remind me I'm saved because of the gift of salvation you've given me freely. In Jesus's name, amen.

DAY 113

In Fellowship, You Are There

When I am with other believers, God is there.

"For where two or three are gathered together in My name, I am there in the midst of them."

—MATTHEW 18:20

Dear Lord, you are among us whenever I am gathered in fellowship with others in your name. When I am with others praying, you are there with us. When I am sharing my testimony, you are there. When I am with others sharing a meal, you are there with us. You are constantly with me when I am in the company of others. In those encounters, I belong and am reminded that we belong to you. In Jesus's name, amen.

DAY 114

Peacemaker

I want to be a peacemaker in this world.

Blessed *are* the peacemakers,
For they shall be called sons of God.

—MATTHEW 5:9

Dear heavenly Father, this world is charged with tension and conflict. Yet you call your children to be peacemakers. Use moments of peace to open conversations about Jesus and turn people's hearts toward you. Focus my heart on the bright and joyful aspects of your creation and break my heart for those in need. Let me help carry the burdens that others carry. Let these glimmers of light redeem and become an antidote to harsher moments that we can encounter. In Jesus's name, amen.

DAY 115

Trusting Through Fear

God's love is greater than anxiety.

Be anxious for nothing, but in everything by prayer and supplication, with thanksgiving, let your requests be made known to God . . .

—PHILIPPIANS 4:6

Whenever I am afraid,
I will trust in You.

—PSALM 56:3

Dear God, in the moments before Jesus went to the cross, he could've let his anxiety take over, but instead, he brought his pain and struggle to you in prayer. He begged for the cup to be taken from him, and ultimately surrendered his will to yours. Whenever I face anxiety, remind me that you are with me even when I'm afraid. In Jesus's name, amen.

DAY 116

Do Everything in Love

I want to glorify the Lord with my work.

And whatever you do, do it heartily, as to the Lord and not to men, knowing that from the Lord you will receive the reward of the inheritance; for you serve the Lord Christ.

—COLOSSIANS 3:23–24

Dear God, help me see every part of my life as worship, whether I'm folding laundry, sending emails, or serving at church. Remind me that all of it is sacred, even the mundane, ordinary, behind-the-scenes tasks, because you intend us to do it all with love and for your glory. And when I feel tired, overwhelmed, or discouraged, give me rest. Help me serve with integrity and purpose in everything I do. You gently redirect my heart back to you. In Jesus's name, amen.

DAY 117

Enduring Temptation

I want to endure everything the enemy throws my way.

Blessed *is* the man who endures temptation; for when he has been approved, he will receive the crown of life which the Lord has promised to those who love Him.

—JAMES 1:12

No temptation has overtaken you except such as is common to man; but God *is* faithful, who will not allow you to be tempted beyond what you are able, but with the temptation will also make the way of escape, that you may be able to bear *it*.

—1 CORINTHIANS 10:13

Dear Father God, help me flee from what doesn't honor you, even if it's subtle like the temptation to gossip, waste time endlessly scrolling, giving in to gluttony, pride, or an unkind thought. You always promise a way out of temptation. Because you are greater than any trap from the enemy, I can be victorious over every temptation. In Jesus's name, amen.

DAY 118

More than a Conqueror

I am more than a conqueror.

Yet in all these things we are more than conquerors through Him who loved us.

—ROMANS 8:37

Dear Father God, you declare me victorious through Christ. Even in suffering, I am not defeated. Earthly victories may fade, but the triumph we have in Jesus is eternal. Let that truth anchor my heart today. Thank you for the unshakable hope and joy I have in you. Praise you, Lord! In Jesus's name I pray, amen.

DAY 119

A Servant Heart

I am called to serve others.

Therefore, my beloved brethren, be steadfast, immovable, always abounding in the work of the Lord, knowing that your labor is not in vain in the Lord.

—1 CORINTHIANS 15:58

Dear God, thank you for equipping me to serve others with the gifts you've given me. Give me a servant's heart to see service as a privilege, not a burden. Help me serve with a heart that isn't looking to be applauded or credited but simply to glorify you. Even when no one notices, remind me I only serve an audience of one. In Jesus's name, amen.

DAY 120

Every Breathing Thing

We are all the same in Christ.

There is neither Jew nor Greek, there is neither slave nor free, there is neither male nor female; for you are all one in Christ Jesus. And if you *are* Christ's, then you are Abraham's seed, and heirs according to the promise.

—GALATIANS 3:28–29

Dear heavenly Father, witnessing division among your creation is disheartening, and I wonder how much we can endure before your Son returns. Lord, my heart breaks for all the hurt in this place, which is immeasurable to the grief you felt when you sent your Son to die for us. Yet you call us to unite because we are all precious in your eyes as your children. Stop the enemy when he uses his tactics to divide us from one another over things that are finite to you—may we each choose grace and forgiveness within our capacity as individuals. Give us the eyes to see each other the way you see us. In Jesus's name, amen.

DAY 121

Flourish

The Holy Spirit is constantly at work within me.

And have put on the new *man* who is renewed in knowledge according to the image of Him who created him . . .

—COLOSSIANS 3:10

Dear Father God, I am a work in progress as long as I am here on earth—you are not finished with me yet. I pray that on the days when I have no clue how you could use me for your glory, that I remember that you began this good work in me and you will bring it to completion, in your perfect timing. This is the only truth I need to give my life meaning. In Jesus's name, amen.

DAY 122

Come, Follow Me

I surrender all to Jesus.

Then Peter said, "See, we have left all and followed You."
So He said to them, "Assuredly, I say to you, there is no one who has left house or parents or brothers or wife or children, for the sake of the kingdom of God, who shall not receive many times more in this present time, and in the age to come eternal life."

—LUKE 18:28-30

Dear Jesus, like the disciples who immediately left everything behind to follow the Messiah, you've invited me to do the same. You're not asking me to give up what's truly good for me, but to surrender whatever hinders me from walking in joy with you. If there's anything I'm holding on to that you want me to release, show me clearly, and give me the strength to walk away. In your everlasting name, amen.

DAY 123

Faithful in the "Little"

Help me to be faithful with even the most mundane parts of life.

He who *is* faithful in *what is* least is faithful also in much; and he who is unjust in *what is* least is unjust also in much.

—LUKE 16:10

Dear God, walk with me, my every day, in the ordinary, and especially in the parts that feel insignificant. Just as Jesus must've spent many years doing the work of a carpenter, the drudgery is actually sacred ground where you're shaping my heart and my character. You see everything I do, no matter how big or small. Lead me to be faithful in the little things as you prepare me to be entrusted with bigger things. In Jesus's name, amen.

DAY 124

Overcoming Self-Righteousness

God resists those who are prideful.

" 'Should you not also have had compassion on your fellow servant, just as I had pity on you?' "

—MATTHEW 18:33

Dear Jesus, the servant who was relieved of his debt through the king's graces quickly forgot the forgiveness he was granted and demanded to be repaid by his debtor. It's easy to rebuke the servant for his hypocrisy and ruthlessness but in reality, I can be the same. I ask for compassion when I am feeling desperate and broken, yet I am quick to judge others. Reveal where my pride becomes an obstacle in extending grace and love to others, which is what we are called to do. Give me a teachable spirit that welcomes your truth and correction. In your name, amen.

DAY 125

The Fear of Love

I have been grafted into the love of the Father.

For you did not receive the spirit of bondage again to fear, but you received the Spirit of adoption by whom we cry out, "Abba, Father."

—ROMANS 8:15

Dear God, your love is safe, but I can be afraid to receive it. Heal me from the fear that I'm unworthy of your love. Remind me that it's safe to be vulnerable with you and there are no strings attached to your love. You've adopted me, as your child. May I experience your perfect love so profoundly that I will never lose sight of that deep love. In Jesus's name, amen.

DAY 126

Fear Not

I have confidence in the Lord because he is always with me.

" 'Fear not, for I *am* with you;
Be not dismayed, for I *am* your God.
I will strengthen you,
Yes, I will help you,
I will uphold you with My righteous right hand.' "

—ISAIAH 41:10

Dear heavenly Father, I thank you that every single day, I can put my confidence in you, even when I don't know what's ahead. When I feel stuck in fear, doubt, and procrastination, I hold myself back from being fully how you've intended me to be. Remind me, in those moments, that I don't have to figure everything out on my own. When hesitation creeps in, you're right by my side. In Jesus's name, amen.

DAY 127

Count the Cost

Would I give up everything for Christ?

"If anyone comes to Me and does not hate his father and mother, wife and children, brothers and sisters, yes, and his own life also, he cannot be My disciple. And whoever does not bear his cross and come after Me cannot be My disciple."

—LUKE 14:26–27

Heavenly Father, make me just like Jesus, who knew the cross was your will, and understood that the cost to following you would bring discomfort, rejection, and ridicule. You ask for total commitment—to blindly follow you. Give me a heart that's fully devoted to you. Because Jesus endured and overcame any challenge he faced, he demonstrates to me that I can follow in the same way and trust in the joy and safety of the promises that are waiting for me. In Jesus's name, amen.

DAY 128

Exceedingly Abundant

God can do anything!

Now to Him who is able to do exceedingly abundantly above all that we ask or think, according to the power that works in us . . .

—EPHESIANS 3:20

Heavenly Father, I come to you in prayer with fears, especially when my circumstances seem beyond what I can handle and worries feel too big to manage. Forgive me for doubting and forgetting that your power is, in fact, limitless. May I know that your plans are mobilized to do immeasurably more than what I imagine. Give me the confidence and the boldness to shout for help. Comfort my heart to know that you can take it from here, infinitely beyond my limited capacity. What a relief to know that you will one day relieve me of my burdens. Thank you! In Jesus's name, amen.

DAY 129

Godly Confidence

I can have godly confidence in all things.

But when they deliver you up, do not worry about how or what you should speak. For it will be given to you in that hour what you should speak; for it is not you who speak, but the Spirit of your Father who speaks in you.

—MATTHEW 10:19–20

Dear Jesus, I can walk in boldness every single day because I have confidence that God will give me the words even when it isn't comfortable. I might find myself in settings where I feel like an outsider, but you put me there for a purpose. Give me godly confidence, not in myself, but from trusting that the Spirit of my Father will speak through me. In your name, amen.

DAY 130

Washed Clean and Set Free from Guilt

Jesus has washed me clean, I have no place for guilt.

Let us draw near with a true heart in full assurance of faith, having our hearts sprinkled from an evil conscience and our bodies washed with pure water.

—HEBREWS 10:22

Dear Lord, thank you for washing me pure of guilt through Jesus's sacrifice, that in your eyes, I am as white as snow (Psalm 51:7). Thank you for reminding me that once I've repented I don't need to keep carrying the weight of regret, because you've already set me free. Help me let go of what you've already taken away, so I can fully step into the calling you've placed on my life. Give me peace and the freedom to walk today with joy and lightness! In Jesus's name, amen.

DAY 131

God Always Answers

Seek the Lord, he is listening.

I sought the LORD, and He heard me,
And delivered me from all my fears.

—PSALM 34:4

Dear God, thank you for hearing each of my prayers, no matter how lacking in eloquence or clumsy they might sound. You always respond. You comfort me and you're still there. Even in moments of silence or doubt. Anything I face is never too great for you, and you never turn me away when I seek you. When I stumble with how to pray, all I have to do is try. Will you give me the courage to say "Dear Father" today? In Jesus's name, amen.

DAY 132

Eternal Life

Eternal life is found in Christ.

And this is eternal life, that they may know You, the only true God, and Jesus Christ whom You have sent.

—JOHN 17:3

Dear Abba Father, thank you for sending Jesus to die on the cross to make a way for me to spend eternity with you. What a miraculous blessing that it is a free gift to those who confess Jesus as Lord. Help me to remember that you are with me on this journey of faith and as long as I look at you beside me, I know that I am aligned with you. In Jesus's name, amen.

DAY 133

Satisfy My Thirst

I want to give my emotional emptiness to Jesus.

O God, You *are* my God;
Early will I seek You;
My soul thirsts for You;
My flesh longs for You
In a dry and thirsty land
Where there is no water.
So I have looked for You in the sanctuary,
To see Your power and Your glory.

—PSALM 63:1–2

Dear Lord, there are times when heaviness presses into me, and I am lonely and emotionally drained. In this dry place, show me what is at the root of my emptiness. I want to give you my burdens so you can lift them off my shoulders. Even when it feels like the impossible, I want to believe that you are capable to be the reprieve I need. When I struggle with unbelief and doubt, please lead me closer to you. In Jesus's name, amen.

DAY 134

The Purpose of Prayer

I want my heart aligned with the Father's.

However, the report went around concerning Him all the more; and great multitudes came together to hear, and to be healed by Him of their infirmities. So He Himself *often* withdrew into the wilderness and prayed.

—LUKE 5:15-16

Dear Jesus, thank you for showing me that prayer is not just a ritual, but a place of deep connection with you. Even when crowds of people came looking for healing, you didn't let their demands distract you from staying centered on the power of prayer. I often pray to ask for a change in my circumstances, but you invite me into a deeper purpose, which is to change me. Remind me of this so my heart can be realigned with yours. In your powerful name, amen.

DAY 135

Jesus Understands My Pain

I never face my pain alone.

For we do not have a High Priest who cannot sympathize with our weaknesses, but was in all *points* tempted as *we are, yet* without sin. Let us therefore come boldly to the throne of grace, that we may obtain mercy and find grace to help in time of need.

—HEBREWS 4:15-16

Dear heavenly Father, I am comforted knowing Jesus understands everything I go through. As both God and human, he experienced deep emotions and pain. He himself was wounded, rejected, and beaten. You empathize with my pain, and you invite me to enter your throne room of grace for anything I need. Because of that, I never have to face anything alone. You've never once left me and never will. Thank you for your constant presence and healing. In Jesus's name, amen.

DAY 136

Growing in Your Will

God's will is for my sanctification.

That you may walk worthy of the Lord, fully pleasing *Him*, being fruitful in every good work and increasing in the knowledge of God; strengthened with all might, according to His glorious power, for all patience and longsuffering with joy . . .

—COLOSSIANS 1:10-11

Dear Abba Father, to believe in you is to strive to be more like you. I see Paul's life and his committed, loving devotion to you, but I confess that I can struggle to see what that means and looks like for me, especially in today's world. Please see my earnest and willing heart, renew my thoughts to see and accept the ordinary as powerful opportunities to learn and grow more like you in each waking moment. In Jesus's name, amen.

DAY 137

Forgiving Others

Extending God's forgiveness to others.

Then Peter came to Him and said, "Lord, how often shall my brother sin against me, and I forgive him? Up to seven times?"
Jesus said to him, "I do not say to you, up to seven times, but up to seventy times seven."

—MATTHEW 18:21-22

Dear Lord, naturally, I want to pull away from those who've hurt me out of self-protection, or to seek justice in my own way. Show me how to forgive others just as you've forgiven me. Expand my perspective to see that we are all works in progress. Jesus demonstrated that forgiveness shows others the same love and grace you've shown me. You are working in all of our hearts. May the way I forgive point others back to your love. In Jesus's name, amen.

DAY 138

God, You are Radiant

The Lord is radiant.

They looked to Him and were radiant,
And their faces were not ashamed.

—PSALM 34:5

Dear Father God, when I spend time in your presence in prayer, worship, and the Word, I am overwhelmed by your glory and majesty. You are as radiant as the sun, full of glory, honor, and power, and I'm inspired to sing my heart out in praise. Any true encounter with your presence fills my heart with peace and strength. May this sense of wonder stay alive in me. In Jesus's name, amen.

DAY 139

God's Favor

Favor surrounds me like a shield.

For You, O Lord, will bless the righteous;
With favor You will surround him as *with* a shield.

—PSALM 5:12

Dear Lord, your favor surrounds me like a shield. Your protection is a constant presence that guards me, even when I am not aware of the battles that are present or the ones that lie ahead. You actively fight for me, and it is through your love and favor that I can stand upright. I am chosen by you and thank you for your faithful love. In Jesus's name I pray, amen.

DAY 140

Be a Light

I shine as a light in this world, not laboring in vain.

Do all things without complaining and disputing, that you may become blameless and harmless, children of God without fault in the midst of a crooked and perverse generation, among whom you shine as lights in the world, holding fast the word of life, so that I may rejoice in the day of Christ that I have not run in vain or labored in vain.

—PHILIPPIANS 2:14–16

Dear God, when I'm tempted to complain, flood my heart with your love so that it illuminates your perfect provision in my life. Give me the comfort I need, and more importantly, a good attitude, a grateful heart, and the maturity to respond in grace and humility even when it's hard. In Jesus's name, amen.

DAY 141

A Faithful Garden

The Holy Spirit is constantly cultivating the soil of my soul.

For as the earth brings forth its bud,
As the garden causes the things that are sown in it to spring forth,
So the Lord God will cause righteousness and praise to spring forth before all the nations.

—ISAIAH 61:11

Dear God, it is my prayer that you will cultivate the soil of my soul to be fruitful. I see my life as a garden, and you will weed out anything that doesn't align with you. Make room for the plans you have for me to blossom in my life. You have beautiful plans for me, and I am eager to watch your work actively change me. Thank you for purifying my heart. In Jesus's name, amen.

DAY 142

Fruit of the Spirit

I want the fruit of the spirit to be present in my life.

But the fruit of the Spirit is love, joy, peace, longsuffering, kindness, goodness, faithfulness, gentleness, self-control. Against such there is no law.

—GALATIANS 5:22-23

Dear Father God, as a branch draws life from the vine, let my relationship with you be fruitful. By your Spirit, grow in me a joy and peace untouched by changing circumstances, patience that waits on your perfect timing, kindness and goodness toward others, steadfast faithfulness to being connected to you, humble meekness when I feel entitled, and self-control in the midst of temptations. In Jesus's name, amen.

DAY 143

Establish My Thoughts

Commit your ways to the Lord, and he will lead you.

"'Call to Me, and I will answer you, and show you great and mighty things, which you do not know.'"

—JEREMIAH 33:3

Dear God, nothing is too small or too big for you. You desire to be with me at every moment; even when it's as simple as brushing my teeth in the morning or thinking about how my day might unfold, you desire to be in conversation with me. Please shape my thoughts to guide and empower me. I entrust you with my week—every task, every meeting, and every decision to be made. In each step I take, I trust that it is in your provision. In Jesus's name, amen.

DAY 144

Dwell in the Secret Place

I am safe.

He who dwells in the secret place of the Most High shall abide under the shadow of the Almighty.

—PSALM 91:1

Dear heavenly Father, when I put my trust in you, I am safe. When I want to give up and my heart feels restless, you bring me to a quiet place under your wings. It's in stillness that I can hear what you have in store for me. You calm my thoughts and remind me of who you are. You speak wisdom, peace, and hope into my life. Thank you for keeping me hidden and protected when I need a retreat from the world. In Jesus's name, amen.

DAY 145

Surrendered Dreams

I commit my hopes and dreams to the Lord,
trusting he will bring them to pass.

Commit your works to the LORD,
And your thoughts will be established.

—PROVERBS 16:3

Dear heavenly Father, you've planted so many hopes and dreams in my heart—I thank you for the gift of creativity! I know you will open the right doors, close the wrong ones, and bring the relationships that fit into your plan. I commit my hopes and dreams to you. What you ultimately have planned for me is better than anything I could've planned for myself. Let your glory, not my own success, be my highest goal. In Jesus's name, amen.

DAY 146

Choosing the Narrow Way

I want to choose what's right, even when it's difficult.

"Enter by the narrow gate; for wide *is* the gate and broad *is* the way that leads to destruction, and there are many who go in by it. Because narrow *is* the gate and difficult *is* the way which leads to life, and there are few who find it.

—MATTHEW 7:13-14

Dear Jesus, I feel alone and misunderstood at times, especially when it seems like I'm living differently from the world. You said that few will choose the narrow way, the path that leads to life. When I choose honesty instead of what's easy or forgive people who hurt me, it can feel unnatural and even isolating. But you remind me that the path is lonely because few walk it. Help me stay faithful even when it's hard. I'm never alone because you're always with me. In your name, amen.

DAY 147

No More Condemnation

Guilt is from the enemy.

For God did not send His Son into the world to condemn the world, but that the world through Him might be saved.

—JOHN 3:17

Dear Lord, when I hear the voice of condemnation, I feel unworthy and like a failure. Help me discern your gentle voice when you reveal that a change is needed in me. Whenever I feel irredeemable, release my shame. Even if my mistakes cannot be reversed, give me the strength to not stay in this place. Teach me to depend on you and release my burdens. You didn't send Jesus for us to stew in our guilt and grievances; he came as a light so we can freely be close to you and experience your goodness. I turn to your loving correction and restoration. In Jesus's name, amen.

DAY 148

Dwell in His Presence

I want to dwell with God.

One *thing* I have desired of the LORD,
That will I seek:
That I may dwell in the house of the LORD
All the days of my life,
To behold the beauty of the LORD,
And to inquire in His temple.

—PSALM 27:4

Dear Father God, I desire to dwell with you always, not just when I need an urgent prayer answered. I want to make my home in your presence so I can witness all that you're capable of in every moment. I want to greet you in heaven in eternity where Jesus has prepared a place for me. In Jesus's name, amen.

DAY 149

True Greatness

I never know what someone else is facing.

They said to Him, "Grant us that we may sit, one on Your right hand and the other on Your left, in Your glory."
But Jesus said to them, "You do not know what you ask. Are you able to drink the cup that I drink, and be baptized with the baptism that I am baptized with?"

—MARK 10:37-38

Dear heavenly Father, greatness isn't about being on a platform under the spotlight or having influence over others, but I get swept up in how perfect and enviable their lives seem, even when I know it's an illusion. Redirect my focus from who gets a seat of honor by the world's standards to firmly being where you call me to be. Jesus challenges us to examine what it means to truly be a humble servant. Grow my spirit to seek your true kingdom. In Jesus's name, amen.

DAY 150

Progress Over Perfectionism

I am constantly growing toward becoming like Jesus.

Not that I have already attained, or am already perfected; but I press on, that I may lay hold of that for which Christ Jesus has also laid hold of me.

—PHILIPPIANS 3:12

Dear Lord, I pray against the grip of perfectionism. Help me trust the process of becoming more like Jesus, even when progress feels slow or messy. Help me see the progress I've made, even small signs of growth, because you're not done with me yet. I'm under construction, being shaped daily by your grace. As long as there's breath in my lungs, you're renewing my mind and transforming me from the inside out. Give me strength to press on toward the life you've called me to live. In Jesus's name, amen.

DAY 151

Peace in Chaos

Confusion is not from God.

For God is not *the author* of confusion but of peace, as in all the churches of the saints.

—1 CORINTHIANS 14:33

Dear Jesus, when you came to be among the brokenhearted, you sat with the weary, lost, and sick. You used your position to make others feel known, loved, and seen. The power we have to carry and give peace isn't created from our own efforts, it's one you've perfectly demonstrated. Thank you for seeing me. In your name, amen

DAY 152

Be Intentional

Be intentional in your planning.

The plans of the diligent *lead* surely to plenty,
But *those of* everyone *who is* hasty, surely to poverty.

—PROVERBS 21:5

Dear Father God, I am impatient and pursue a vision for my life that I've determined by my own calculations. But you're a God who is intentional about your plans for my life. Refine me to slow down in this ambitious but fruitless chase, so that I can invite you to be with me in my every move. You see me when I follow my own judgments, but I am thankful that you are patient and you work in your own timeline. Give me a deliberating heart to walk with you with intention. In Jesus's name, amen.

DAY 153

Power Over Sin

I have the power of Jesus living inside of me.

And do not lead us into temptation,
But deliver us from the evil one.

—MATTHEW 6:13

Dear Jesus, you told the disciples to pray against temptation because you know sin can weaken our defenses and keep us distant from you. The enemy wants to damage my witness and dim my passion. Please stop sin from ruling my thoughts, emotions, and actions. When I'm tempted to find comfort in shortcuts, remind me that your power is available to me the moment I call on you. In your glorious name, amen.

DAY 154

Freedom from Sin

Forgive me of my sins, Lord.

If we say that we have no sin, we deceive ourselves, and the truth is not in us. If we confess our sins, He is faithful and just to forgive us *our* sins and to cleanse us from all unrighteousness.

—1 JOHN 1:8–9

Dear God, I come to you today as I am. In my flaws, I confess I hold on to ways that aren't according to what you taught. I act with pride, speak without kindness, withhold love, hide in comfort, or carry resentment. But because of the cross, I am able to walk out in your freedom at the start of each new day. You restore me and give me a fresh chance to be free from guilt and to grow in your goodness. Thank you, in Jesus's name, amen.

DAY 155

God Multiplies

We serve a God of multiplication.

And when He had taken the five loaves and the two fish, He looked up to heaven, blessed and broke the loaves, and gave *them* to His disciples to set before them; and the two fish He divided among *them* all. So they all ate and were filled. And they took up twelve baskets full of fragments and of the fish. Now those who had eaten the loaves were about five thousand men.

—MARK 6:41–44

Dear Father God, my strength, time, or gifts don't seem sufficient as an offering. You ask us to surrender whatever we have, no matter how little, with faith. It's Jesus who took five loaves and two fish and fed thousands, and you can do the same with whatever I have, multiplying what I place in your hands for your glory. I lay down my pride, and offer what I have to you with open hands and heart. In Jesus's name, amen.

DAY 156

UNITED TO HONOR

I am united with my brothers and sisters in Christ.

Now I plead with you, brethren, by the name of our Lord Jesus Christ, that you all speak the same thing, and *that* there be no divisions among you, but *that* you be perfectly joined together in the same mind and in the same judgment.

—1 CORINTHIANS 1:10

Dear heavenly Father, while I try to focus on all the goodness you provide, conflict and clashing opinions can creep into personal conversations, everyday interactions, and even my relationships. When I have a difference in views or opinions with others, keep our hearts centered on you, so that we may honor each other. You have breathed life into every single one of us, bless us so we can see you in one another. In Jesus's name, amen.

DAY 157

TRUE JOY

Rejoicing brings joy.

Therefore you now have sorrow; but I will see you again and your heart will rejoice, and your joy no one will take from you.

—JOHN 16:22

Dear God, help me to see the counterfeit "joys" of this world for exactly what they are, knowing they will leave me empty and unfulfilled. You don't ask me to overlook my desires or dismiss them as petty. But please mature my heart so I can seek out things beyond worldly comforts, and also open my heart to feel deeply the joy that you offer. In Jesus's name, amen.

DAY 158

FLOURISH

The Lord allows me to flourish.

May the LORD give you increase more and more,
You and your children.

—PSALM 115:14

Dear God, through you, everything is possible. I go through each day, uncertain about where it's all leading to, if I'll amount to anything significant, or if my contributions are worthwhile. But you command that what I do serves your great work, even if it might be unclear to me at this moment. Give me the clarity to see that I am a part of your great work. In Jesus's name, amen.

DAY 159

FILL ME AGAIN AND AGAIN

God will fill me up again and again.

"But you shall receive power when the Holy Spirit has come upon you; and you shall be witnesses to Me in Jerusalem, and in all Judea and Samaria, and to the end of the earth."

—ACTS 1:8

And do not be drunk with wine, in which is dissipation; but be filled with the Spirit . . .

—EPHESIANS 5:18

Dear heavenly Father, I need you, not just every day but through every moment of each day. Fill my cup so I may be attuned with you. I am promised strength from a source that's not mine, and from a power that flows from you. Replenish me so that your Spirit may work through me in ways I never could on my own. In Jesus's name, amen.

DAY 160

Discerning Truth

Allow me to be wise in learning.

Beloved, do not believe every spirit, but test the spirits, whether they are of God; because many false prophets have gone out into the world.

—1 JOHN 4:1

Dear Lord, sharpen my ability to discern between true wisdom that comes from you and wisdom that only sounds good on the surface. Open my eyes, ears, and heart to what you want me to see. When I'm not sure, bring me to your word so I can be reminded of your steadfast and loving nature. Remind me that I can meet you through prayer, and Scripture is always there when I seek your voice. I can revisit familiar teachings to discover new meanings and intricate truths. I am surrounded by all I need, and you reveal what being wise means through your eyes, thank you! Align me in your steps. In Jesus's name, amen.

DAY 161

A Life-Giving Tongue

May my words bring health to the listener.

Pleasant words *are like* a honeycomb,
Sweetness to the soul and health to the bones.

—PROVERBS 16:24

Dear heavenly Father, I want to be a light to everyone I encounter. I want to share life-giving words to others so they can experience nourishment to their soul and health to their bones. Shape my heart and fill it with kindness, compassion, and wisdom so that my words flow from a heart anchored in your love. Give me encouraging, healing, and truthful words to speak to others that glorify you. In Jesus's name, amen.

DAY 162

Victory Through Christ

Free from shame, victorious in Christ.

But thanks *be* to God,
who gives us the victory through our Lord Jesus Christ.

—1 CORINTHIANS 15:57

Dear Jesus, you are the gift to us from God. In my day to day, I pray for your help and ask for what I need. I confess it doesn't always come easy to turn to you and think of eternal life; it can feel lofty and far away. But remind me that I can choose you each day with faith, love, kindness, and that is the hope I can cling on to and celebrate. In your name I pray, amen.

DAY 163

Rest Awhile

Take rest and find renewal.

And He said to them, "Come aside by yourselves to a deserted place and rest a while." For there were many coming and going, and they did not even have time to eat.

—MARK 6:31

Dear Jesus, even when your ministry demanded a lot from your disciples, you took the time to see their efforts. You acknowledged their limits and need for rest. You demonstrated that taking time away to reset, recover, and reconnect were essential and part of your good work. You don't encourage or thrive on burnout. You teach us to withdraw, take time, and renew ourselves in body and spirit. Teach me to pause and take rest so that I can continue to keep going. In your name I pray, amen.

DAY 164

For Good

All things work together for good.

And we know that all things work together for good to those who love God, to those who are the called according to *His* purpose.

—ROMANS 8:28

Dear Lord, Joseph was betrayed by his brothers, sold into slavery, falsely accused, and left in prison for over a decade. Yet you used every hardship to preserve the people through whom Jesus would come. What others meant for harm, you used for the redemption of the world. When life feels unfair or delayed, remind me that you are working behind the scenes and I have so much to look forward to. Help me trust that even my pain is part of your purpose. You are always weaving good into every thread of my story. In Jesus's name, amen.

DAY 165

Extending Compassion

I want to bear the burdens of my brothers and sisters in Christ.

Therefore comfort each other and edify one another, just as you also are doing.

—1 THESSALONIANS 5:11

Rejoice with those who rejoice, and weep with those who weep.

—ROMANS 12:15

Dear Lord, I am a sinner, no better than any of my brothers and sisters. We all face different challenges in this life, and I want to be a sister that others can call on to share their burdens with, someone they know will pray for and with them, someone who will stand in the gap for them, and someone who will be uplifting, kind, and honest. Give me guidance to support my family of faith during their difficult times. In Jesus's name, amen.

DAY 166

Heavenly Affection

I want to set my mind on heavenly things.

Set your mind on things above, not on things on the earth.

—COLOSSIANS 3:2

Dear God, I strive to be the best in all that I do, in all roles I have been entrusted with: to be a faithful daughter in Christ, a good friend, a caring family member, an encouraging colleague, a nurturing mother. You see in my heart that I take on these roles with great responsibility and try to the best of my ability to do them well. But I have a tendency to do this to earn approval and love; my mind fills with busy calculations or anxieties. When I start focusing only on what's in front of me, keep my gaze up and turn my thoughts into prayers that I give over to you because I can rest in you. In Jesus's name, amen.

DAY 167

God of Hope

A hope that is rooted in the promise of Jesus's return.

Therefore, having been justified by faith, we have peace with God through our Lord Jesus Christ, through whom also we have access by faith into this grace in which we stand, and rejoice in hope of the glory of God.

—ROMANS 5:1-2

Dear God, all hope is found in you, and through that truth I receive your joy and peace. Life doesn't always feel peaceful or go how I imagined it would, but the promise of renewal anchors me in an outlook that is rooted in eternal life. I thank you for grounding me in a belief that doesn't depend on how things look or feel. It's a hope that is rooted in the promise of Jesus's return. In Jesus's name, amen.

DAY 168

Trust Over Understanding

I trust the Lord, even when I don't understand.

Jesus answered and said to him, "What I am doing you do not understand now, but you will know after this."

—JOHN 13:7

Dear Jesus, you told your disciples there were things they weren't going to understand until later. There are things in my life I don't fully understand yet, and I catch myself trying to figure things out. I trick myself into thinking that if I can figure out the "why," then I can protect myself from getting hurt or avoid disappointment. When I do this to feel safe or in control, show me that I'm manufacturing a counterfeit peace. Thank you for lovingly and gently leading me back to your peace. In your mighty name, amen.

DAY 169

Freedom from Bondage

I was set free from the bondage of sin.

And having been set free from sin, you became slaves of righteousness.

—ROMANS 6:18

Dear heavenly Father, thank you for redeeming me from sin. Being in a relationship with you gives me peace and a new life. You say being freed from sin isn't permission for me to have free rein over my life, it means following your guidance. Learning from Jesus is to choose God's yoke, which is easy and its burden light. May I glorify your name in all that I do. In Jesus's name, amen.

DAY 170

Mercy Not Stones

I want to love mercy.

"Judge not, and you shall not be judged. Condemn not, and you shall not be condemned. Forgive, and you will be forgiven."

—LUKE 6:37

Dear God, your word tells me to love mercy, to be compassionate even when punishing or judging them may feel like a natural response. Jesus showed us what mercy looks like in John 8 when the woman committing adultery was given new life, free from shame and condemnation. You choose to show me the same generosity so I can know the love of Christ. In Jesus's name, amen.

DAY 171

Captivated

I am captivated by the Lord; I behold his beauty.

And the Word became flesh and dwelt among us, and we beheld His glory, the glory as of the only begotten of the Father, full of grace and truth.

—JOHN 1:14

Dear Jesus, you are the King of Kings, yet your throne is always approachable. You wash the feet of fishermen and tax collectors. You calm storms, raise the dead, and speak words that stir my soul. Though Scripture says your physical appearance was plain by the world's standards, I am captivated by your beauty. I long to be with you and bow in awe and gratitude. In your name, amen.

DAY 172

Giving Him Thanks

Declaring my gratitude is faith.

And one of them, when he saw that he was healed, returned, and with a loud voice glorified God, and fell down on *his* face at His feet, giving Him thanks. And he was a Samaritan.

—LUKE 17:15-16

Dear heavenly Father, what a miracle it is to wake up each day with new life! When Jesus healed ten men with leprosy, one came back in health to give thanks for renewal. I don't want to assume that you know my grateful heart. I want to come to you at each moment to express gratitude for my wholeness as a reminder that my faith has made me well. In Jesus's name, amen.

DAY 173

A Personal Invitation

Because I believe in the Lord, I will not face condemnation.

"He who believes in Him is not condemned; but he who does not believe is condemned already, because he has not believed in the name of the only begotten Son of God."

—JOHN 3:18

Dear God, sometimes it's easier to believe that Jesus died on the cross for the whole world, than to believe he did it personally for me. But when I sit with the knowledge that you personally invite each one of us into a relationship with you, I can start to believe that your love is as fierce and personal for me as it is for anyone else. Thank you for knowing me and making me unique in your image. In Jesus's name, amen.

DAY 174

Weariness

Give your weariness to him.

"For My yoke *is* easy and My burden is light."

—MATTHEW 11:30

Dear Lord, I'm often uncertain about what it would look like to truly release my burdens to you. I come to you and ask for you to take the weight away, but I often still hold tight on to it. Forgive my unbelief even when you promise that your burden is light! Help me relinquish control to you daily, to lay everything at the foot of the cross and boldly choose you. In Jesus's name, amen.

DAY 175

Glory in Nature

God's glory is in all things.

The heavens declare the glory of God;
And the firmament shows His handiwork.

—PSALM 19:1

Dear heavenly Father, your glory is the sunrise and the sunset. I see it in a child's laugh and birds in the sky. I see your glory as I sit on the beach and watch the tide roll in and out. Your glory is the rain falling from the sky, and as I experience the beauty of passing seasons each and every year, your glory is woven throughout creation. Give me eyes to see it each and every day. In Jesus's name, amen.

DAY 176

Beauty Is Fleeting

Physical beauty isn't everything.

Charm *is* deceitful, and beauty *is* passing,
But a woman *who* fears the Lord, she shall be praised.

—PROVERBS 31:30

Dear heavenly Father, the world has a moving target for ideals and I confess, I am easily swayed. I compare my looks, intellect, how much money I have, how put together I present myself, and how perfect my relationships or home looks. And I can feel brief confidence when I give in to those influences. But it is all fleeting and comparing is a trap that becomes impossible to untangle from. In those moments, remind me: You plainly accept me with zero conditions, and I am your own. Help me to remember the satisfaction of receiving your pure, whole embrace. In Jesus's name, amen.

DAY 177

Obeying From Love

I love the Lord; I want to be obedient to him.

"If you love Me, keep My commandments."

—JOHN 14:15

Dear God, being obedient can stir up fears of failing or uncertainty about walking out boldly in faith. You are a kind Father who pursues and encourages me to carry out the purposes you have for my life rather than a demanding taskmaster. Refine the gifts you have entrusted in me to nurture my faith so that I may take good care of what you've trusted me with and experience more of the love that you freely give. In Jesus's name, amen.

DAY 178

Conquering Fear

God has given me all I need to combat fear.

For God has not given us a spirit of fear, but of power and of love and of a sound mind.

—2 TIMOTHY 1:7

Dear Lord, sometimes my fears flow like a leaking faucet—whether they are fears about financial strain, my health status, or the state of the world. Shut the faucet of fear off in my life and flood me instead with your power, love, and a sound mind. When I can't see the whole picture, remind me your way is always better than mine. I have everything I need to conquer my fear because the Spirit living in me is greater than any threat in this world. In Jesus's name, amen.

DAY 179

The Blessing of Family

Being together brings joy.

Two *are* better than one,
Because they have a good reward for their labor.
For if they fall, one will lift up his companion.
But woe to him *who is* alone when he falls,
For *he has* no one to help him up.

—ECCLESIASTES 4:9-10

Dear Lord, thank you for giving us the priceless gift of family. Whether we are linked by blood, or chosen by love, we thrive when we are in community with one another. They lift me up when I need support, we celebrate each other's successes, and they keep me company in seasons of loneliness. Help me cherish each one of them so I never lose sight of how much they mean to me—and so they may know it too. In Jesus's name, amen.

DAY 180

Seeking You First

I want to seek the Lord above all else.

Seek the LORD while He may be found,
Call upon Him while He is near.

—ISAIAH 55:6

Dear heavenly Father, when the demands of every day pull me in different directions, I forget you're right there. You promise that if I seek you with all of my heart, I'll find you. All I need to do is call your name! Let my first and last moments in each day and every moment in between be in your presence so I can notice the tender ways you pursue connection with me. In Jesus's name, amen.

DAY 181

Two Small Coins

Create in me a generous heart.

Then one poor widow came and threw in two mites, which make a quadrans.

—MARK 12:42

Dear Jesus, you saw the widow's offering not by the monetary worth but from her heart posture, ready to surrender everything she had for your glory. You don't ask for lavish gifts or performative acts of devotion. You see and love us in the unseen acts of love or small gestures of kindness and heartfelt offerings. Jesus, you remind me that you see me, you know me, and you love me. Thank you, in your name, amen.

DAY 182

Growth in Trials

I want to have joy in all circumstances.

My brethren, count it all joy when you fall into various trials, knowing that the testing of your faith produces patience.

—JAMES 1:2-3

Dear heavenly Father, in trials I ask you, "Why this? Why now?" And I often don't understand why you allow certain tests even when I am in pain. Mature my heart so I can see that you are not only a witness to my suffering, but you know exactly what I feel. Through it, you are nudging me to grow my faith and patience through these challenges. And when I am hesitant, remind me that you're exposing my heart to grow, expanding my gratitude, cultivating my confidence in your goodness, and helping me surrender every part of my life to your grace. In Jesus's name, amen.

DAY 183

From Pain to Purpose

God is my ultimate comforter.

Blessed *be* the God and Father of our Lord Jesus Christ, the Father of mercies and God of all comfort, who comforts us in all our tribulation, that we may be able to comfort those who are in any trouble, with the comfort with which we ourselves are comforted by God.

—2 CORINTHIANS 1:3-4

Dear heavenly Father, you have comforted me and carried me in trouble. Through my trials, you stretched my heart and gave me a deeper ability for empathy and understanding to extend to others. Thank you for calling me to encourage others who've walked through similar valleys. My pain was not in vain; I know you are shaping me and will use my overcoming to bring healing and comfort to others. In Jesus's name, amen.

DAY 184

Victory Through Faith

I will overcome this world.

For whatever is born of God overcomes the world. And this is the victory that has overcome the world—our faith.

—1 JOHN 5:4

Dear God, I am your child and through Jesus, I have a new identity in him. In my daily life, battles mean the struggles of waiting, loneliness, doubt, and stress. But your word says that having faith is the victory! I am victorious because I trust in you. In Jesus's name, amen.

DAY 185

Lord, Help me!

When I am struggling, the Lord helps me.

Peace I leave with you, My peace I give to you; not as the world gives do I give to you. Let not your heart be troubled, neither let it be afraid.

—JOHN 14:27

Heavenly Father, whenever I'm struggling, I focus on keeping up with everything I need to accomplish—errands, responsibilities I need to fulfill, maintaining relationships, checking off my to-dos. When I pause, I can remember that you care about my burdens, you help carry the weight no matter what I'm going through. I can seek your help to change my situation or expand my perspective toward what I'm going through. When I call on you, you always respond. I want to believe and receive your power as it's always available to me. In Jesus's name, amen.

DAY 186

Lavished with Love

The Lord softens my heart with his love.

"I will arise and go to my father, and will say to him, 'Father, I have sinned against heaven and before you, and I am no longer worthy to be called your son. Make me like one of your hired servants.'"

"And he arose and came to his father. But when he was still a great way off, his father saw him and had compassion, and ran and fell on his neck and kissed him."

—LUKE 15:18–20

Dear Father, you're the father who runs toward me with compassion. Your love for me is not dependent on my behavior. The father in the parable of the prodigal son joyfully comes to meet his sons exactly where they are, in their shame and bitterness. You show in this lesson that the reunion and returning home is a moment for celebration and rejoicing! Your promise to us is the greater picture. In Jesus's name, amen.

DAY 187

Satisfied in You Alone

When the path forward is uncertain, I am certain of God's love for me.

"Blessed *is* she who believed, for there will be a fulfillment of those things which were told her from the Lord."

—LUKE 1:45

Dear Father, when young and pregnant Mary visited Elizabeth, Elizabeth was moved by Mary's willing heart to trust wholeheartedly to be your servant and celebrated the Good News of Jesus's coming. Please give me a heart like both Mary and Elizabeth's to courageously follow you without any hesitation, even when the steps forward are uncertain. When I feel lost, surround me with this same certainty and other sisters of faith who can also speak life and blessings to me so I can do the same for others. In Jesus's name, amen.

DAY 188

Running on Empty

I don't want to be so busy that I miss my purpose.

But Martha was distracted with much serving, and she approached Him and said, "Lord, do You not care that my sister has left me to serve alone? Therefore tell her to help me."
And Jesus answered and said to her, "Martha, Martha, you are worried and troubled about many things. But one thing is needed, and Mary has chosen that good part, which will not be taken away from her."

—LUKE 10:40-42

Dear heavenly Father, I try to focus on doing good things but often feel overwhelmed and find myself with a withholding heart rather than overflowing with love and generosity. I often feel the pressure to perform and before I know it, I'm spiritually dry and burnt-out. I get caught up in serving and striving in ways that look fruitful on the outside but leave me depleted on the inside. More than anything, you want my heart. Help me slow down, take rest when I need a break, and replenish my soul. In Jesus's name, amen.

DAY 189

Choosing Your Way This Time

I serve a God of second chances.

Now it was told King David, saying, "The Lord has blessed the house of Obed-Edom and all that *belongs* to him, because of the ark of God." So David went and brought up the ark of God from the house of Obed-Edom to the City of David with gladness. And so it was, when those bearing the ark of the Lord had gone six paces, that he sacrificed oxen and fatted sheep.

—2 SAMUEL 6:12-13

Dear God, I don't always carry your presence with the reverence you deserve or seek your direction. Even when I get it wrong, you never cast me aside. Help me to be like David, who didn't give up because he made a mistake, but learned by trying again in your way. In Jesus's name, amen.

DAY 190

Follow Me

I want to respond to your call with a "yes."

Then He said to them, "Follow Me, and I will make you fishers of men." They immediately left *their* nets and followed Him.

—MATTHEW 4:19–20

Dear Lord Jesus, I am used to being comfortable, stagnant in my values, and indifferent in my human ways. When you asked Andrew and Peter to follow you, they immediately left their lives to go with you. Please activate my heart so that it is wholeheartedly ready to say yes, even when I'm not sure what is ahead. You promise to be with me through it all. In your name, amen.

DAY 191

Guard My Heart From Envy

Jealousy is evil in nature.

For where envy and self-seeking *exist*, confusion and every evil thing *are* there.

—JAMES 3:16

Dear heavenly Father, when I focus on what others have and what I lack, it's because I've drifted from you. Remove envious thoughts that make me question whether you love others more than me and blind me to all I already have. When I'm tempted to ask why I don't have the things other people do, help me hold on to the promise that you always supply everything I need and more, for my good, and because you love me. In Jesus's name, amen.

DAY 192

In Awe of God

I am serving God with reverence.

Therefore, since we are receiving a kingdom which cannot be shaken, let us have grace, by which we may serve God acceptably with reverence and godly fear. For our God *is* a consuming fire.

—HEBREWS 12:28–29

Dear heavenly Father, you are unshakable. Give me your strong hope—firmly plant it in my heart—so that I may be fully confident in your Kingdom. I give thanks with my life, not just in words, because you are deserving of awe. Your grace and mercy gives me the security I need. Let my heart overflow with gratitude. In Jesus's name, amen.

DAY 193

Content in Christ

Be content with what you have.

Trust in the LORD, and do good;
Dwell in the land, and feed on His faithfulness.

—PSALM 37:3

Dear God, I want to be content with what you have given me, but more than that, I want to be content simply in you. Even if nothing more is added to my life, may I still be full of joy knowing that all I need is in Jesus. You promise that as I delight in you, you'll meet the deepest desires of my heart. You are a good Father who always gives his children the best gifts. As long as I have you, I lack nothing. In Jesus's name, amen.

DAY 194

When I Can't, God Can

The Lord has me, even through my failures.

Though he fall, he shall not be utterly cast down;
for the LORD upholds *him with* His hand.

—PSALM 37:24

Dear Father God, failure is inevitable, and some days I wonder if I'm able to get anything right. It feels like I fall short in every way, missing the mark when it comes to my relationships, in staying focused on my duties, and I find myself losing my patience. But you remind me that I can bring my weaknesses to you and you'll never cast me aside. What's impossible for me is possible with you. Focus my eyes on you and less on myself and my perceived failures. In Jesus's name, amen.

DAY 195

Ask for Wisdom

Ask God for wisdom, he is faithful to provide.

If any of you lacks wisdom, let him ask of God, who gives to all liberally and without reproach, and it will be given to him.

—JAMES 1:5

Dear God, when I don't have the answers, I come to you. You're always ready to hear my heart and speak into my life. Keep me from leaning on my limited views or the world's advice. Without you, my best ideas will fall short. Give me your understanding in every situation, to see things from your holy and perfect perspective. Thank you for not leaving me to figure everything out myself. In Jesus's name, amen.

DAY 196

Believing God for the Impossible

There is nothing too difficult for God.

Ah, Lord God! Behold, You have made the heavens and the earth by Your great power and outstretched arm. There is nothing too hard for You.

—JEREMIAH 32:17

Dear God, nothing is too difficult for you! I've faced loss, health scares, and seasons of financial strain, all of which felt impossible to overcome. Yet, each became an opportunity to trust you more deeply, even when I couldn't see a way forward. Give me the same belief that Mary had when she saw Jesus's resurrection. You've delivered me before, and I trust you to do it again. When I place everything into your hands, my worry melts away. Whenever I begin to fear, remind me that you are my Protector. In Jesus's name, amen.

DAY 197

Rest in His Presence

I find rest in the presence of God.

And He said, "My presence will go *with you,* and I will give you rest."

—EXODUS 33:14

Dear Lord, too often I run to things of this world to find comfort, but true comfort can only be found in you. Fill me with your Holy Spirit to renew me from the inside out. Anchor my heart to say yes to you, knowing you will fulfill my every need. I can rest in you because when I do, your grace and unconditional love completely satisfies me. Thank you. In Jesus's name, amen.

DAY 198

Genuine Kindness

Create in me a kind heart.

Therefore, as *the* elect of God, holy and beloved, put on tender mercies, kindness, humility, meekness, longsuffering . . .

—COLOSSIANS 3:12

Dear Lord, grow in me a kind heart, to show kindness through action, without seeking anything in return, but simply to love others the way you love me. Give me empathy for those who are hurting and a willingness to step in when someone needs help carrying what's too heavy to do alone. When you nudge me to show kindness, you guide me to meet others where they're at, just as you have done to me. Lead me to share the hope of Jesus so they know they're never alone. In Jesus's name, amen.

DAY 199

Living Water

Jesus is my portion; he is all I need.

And He said to me, "It is done! I am the Alpha and the Omega, the Beginning and the End. I will give of the fountain of the water of life freely to him who thirsts."

—REVELATION 21:6

Dear Lord, encountering Jesus means I no longer need to turn to the world's ways to temporarily satisfy my soul. Remind me that I don't need to seek anything outside of you because you provide everything I need and invite me to drink from the well of eternal life. Your fountain of life is available to me at any time. In my most desperate moments will you teach me that I can simply desire communion with you and I will be fulfilled? In Jesus's name, amen.

DAY 200

No Need to Fear

Even the smallest details of my life matter to him.

Are not two sparrows sold for a copper coin? And not one of them falls to the ground apart from your Father's will. But the very hairs of your head are all numbered. Do not fear therefore; you are of more value than many sparrows.

—MATTHEW 10:29–31

Dear Father, you are both Creator and provider, and nothing escapes your notice. Remind me that I don't need to be afraid because your will is established in perfect wisdom and love. I'm precious to you and even the smallest details of my life matter. When fear starts to rise in me, help me remember that our heavenly Father cares about every aspect of my life. In Jesus's beautiful name, amen.

DAY 201

Connected to the Vine

It is my desire to grow in my relationship with Christ and become more like him.

But grow in the grace and knowledge of our Lord and Savior Jesus Christ.

—2 PETER 3:18

"I am the vine, you *are* the branches. He who abides in Me, and I in him, bears much fruit; for without Me you can do nothing."

—JOHN 15:5

Dear Lord, thank you for inviting me into a personal relationship with you, not a system of rules. You don't ask me to perform for your love, you just desire my heart. Keep me connected to you as I seek your constant presence. Thank you, Jesus, for making this relationship possible through your sacrifice. Help me bear fruit that honors you. In Jesus's name, amen.

DAY 202

Finish Well

I am an overcomer, and I am seated in heavenly places.

To him who overcomes I will grant to sit with Me on My throne, as I also overcame and sat down with My Father on His throne.

—REVELATION 3:21

Dear God, help me to endure hardship with grace, and to trust you through every trial. Strengthen me to finish the race you've set before me, keeping my eyes on Jesus, the author and finisher of my faith. One day, I will receive a crown, not for my glory, but to lay it at your feet in worship. I want my life to be pleasing to you. In Jesus's name, amen.

DAY 203

Breaking Bread in Fellowship

Being in community with fellow believers is a gift from God.

And they continued steadfastly in the apostles' doctrine and fellowship, in the breaking of bread, and in prayers.

—ACTS 2:42

Dear Lord, I am so grateful for the community of fellow Christians you've brought in my life, for the people who love and support me, for loved ones who encourage me, challenge me, pray with me, and grow together. Help us to spur on one another in faith, speak truth in love, and be willing to hold each other accountable with grace. You are present in each encounter, and it is through those meaningful interactions where faith blooms. In Jesus's name, amen.

DAY 204

SHINE YOUR LIGHT

My light cannot be hidden.

"You are the light of the world, A city that is set on a hill cannot be hidden. Nor do they light a lamp and put it under a basket, but on a lampstand, and it gives light to all *who are* in the house. Let your light so shine before men, that they may see your good works and glorify your Father in heaven."

—MATTHEW 5:14-16

Dear heavenly Father, I am a light for you just as the sun rises each day. Let the light shine bright and spread the hope and peace of Jesus. Whether it's through an act of kindness, sharing my testimony, or encouraging one another, I pray the warmth draws them closer to witness how marvelous you are. In Jesus's name, amen.

DAY 205

SUCCESS WITH GOD

God blesses all the work of my hands.

" 'For the LORD your God has blessed you in all the work of your hand. He knows your trudging through this great wilderness. These forty years the LORD your God *has been* with you; you have lacked nothing.' "

—DEUTERONOMY 2:7

Dear Lord, whenever I worry about whether my plans will succeed, it's a sign I've started relying on my own judgments instead of trusting you with the outcome. When I don't see the fruit of my labor, remind me that you're the One who blesses all the work of my hands. What matters most is that you're shaping my heart and that the motives of my heart remain pure. When I succeed, it is in you. In Jesus's name, amen.

DAY 206

Walking in The Spirit

I want to walk in the Spirit at all times.

I say then: Walk in the Spirit, and you shall not fulfill the lust of the flesh.

—GALATIANS 5:16

Then Jesus, being filled with the Holy Spirit, returned from the Jordan and was led by the Spirit into the wilderness.

—LUKE 4:1

Dear heavenly Father, the Holy Spirit is working in my life. When I spend time in the Word, in prayer, or worship, that is when you are waking me up to be attuned to your loving guidance. Tune me in to hear, listen, and obey so that I won't miss any opportunity to hear your voice! In Jesus's name, amen.

DAY 207

Rejoice Always

I can rejoice in every situation.

Rejoice in the Lord always. Again I will say, rejoice!

—PHILIPPIANS 4:4

Dear heavenly Father, I rejoice in you today knowing you love me without conditions or limits. You have forgiven me and set me free of my sins. I feel the overflow of your love and joy when I look toward you. My circumstances melt away in the light of your glory and grace. I can't wait to be with you in eternity but in the meantime, I will rejoice always. Thank you, Lord. In Jesus's name, amen.

DAY 208

Called for Such a Time as This

I am in the right place at the right time in history
to do the work God has called me to.

"For if you remain completely silent at this time, relief and deliverance will arise for the Jews from another place, but you and your father's house will perish. Yet who knows whether you have come to the kingdom for *such* a time as this?"

—ESTHER 4:14

Dear Lord, just as you placed Esther where you wanted her to be, as a queen to protect her people, you've placed me where I am for a specific purpose. Give me the same courage Esther had to fulfill your plans for me, and the strength of Jesus to keep going, even when the path is difficult. When I'm weak, remind me to rely on your strength. Help me resist my doubts and trust that you'll equip me for what you've called me for. Thank you for choosing me as a vessel for your glory. In Jesus's name, amen.

DAY 209

Pleasing God

Jesus was fully devoted to the Father.

"And He who sent Me is with Me. The Father has not left Me alone, for I always do those things that please Him."

—JOHN 8:29

Dear God, thank you for sending Jesus to be the perfect example of obedience. Jesus explains that he was the chosen one to fulfill your mission on earth, and his total surrender to you highlights his unity with you. As Son of God, Jesus served as the ultimate example for living out his true purpose, bearing humiliation and death so that your children could be redeemed. Just as Jesus fully relied on you, I pray that I can also follow his footsteps in full devotion to you. Please guide my every move so you may be pleased. In Jesus's name, amen.

DAY 210

A Generous Woman

Help me to be a blessing in my community.

She stretches out her hands to the distaff,
And her hand holds the spindle.
She extends her hand to the poor,
Yes, she reaches out her hands to the needy.

—PROVERBS 31:19–20

Dear Lord, give me a heart to give freely because your love overflows from me. May I be quick to give, whether it's to a friend or a stranger. Open doors for me to help others through prayer, resources, physical needs, or emotional support. May my giving ultimately lead people to know and feel loved by you. In Jesus's name, amen.

DAY 211

In Your Image

By God's will, everything was created.

"You are worthy, O Lord,
To receive glory and honor and power;
For You created all things,
And by Your will they exist and were created."

—REVELATION 4:11

Dear God, you made me in your image, and in that image, I carry the gift of creativity. When I create, I see a glimpse of who you are. As I take in the beauty around me, inspire me to create with purpose, humility, and joy—always for your glory. In Jesus's name I pray, amen.

DAY 212

Putting God's Kingdom First

I will prioritize my time with God every day.

But seek first the kingdom of God and His righteousness, and all these things shall be added to you.

—MATTHEW 6:33

Dear Lord, what a privilege it is, to know that when I put you first, everything else will fall into place in my life. When I prioritize my time with you in the Word and in prayer instead of rushing into the whirlwind of each day, I relinquish control and make room for your plans. You abundantly add to my life and remind me that true success is found in you alone. Light my heart to always pursue you first before my own desires. In Jesus's name, amen.

DAY 213

Finding Purpose

My purpose has been prepared by God.

For we are His workmanship, created in Christ Jesus for good works, which God prepared beforehand that we should walk in them.

—EPHESIANS 2:10

Dear heavenly Father, thank you for the divine purpose you've set for my life. You've given me a unique mix of gifts, passions, and experiences to prepare me for the good works you've planned for me. Let my actions mirror my relationship with you. My purpose doesn't have to look like anyone else's. You're not expecting perfection nor are you expecting a carbon copy of someone else, but a willing heart to steward what I have, so you can entrust me with more. In Jesus's name, amen.

DAY 214

Made by Jesus

Everything that has been created is from the Lord.

All things were made through Him, and without Him nothing was made that was made.

—JOHN 1:3

Dear God, everything around and in me, every star, every cell, was made by you. From galaxies to the very first breath in my lungs, all creation reflects your intentional design. You sustain the seasons and care for even the smallest sparrow. Nothing exists apart from you. Thank you for the beauty, order, and purpose woven into all you've made. Just as you were intentional about every detail, help me to appreciate all your intricate works. Help me not to take it for granted. In Jesus's name, amen.

DAY 215

Grounded in Faith

Doubt is from the enemy; hope is from the Lord.

But when he saw that the wind *was* boisterous, he was afraid; and beginning to sink he cried out, saying, "Lord, save me!"
And immediately Jesus stretched out *His* hand and caught him, and said to him, "O you of little faith, why did you doubt?" And when they got into the boat, the wind ceased.

—MATTHEW 14:30-32

Dear God, when doubt creeps in, I question your love, your plans, and whether you really care for me. When it's hard to believe you have my best interest at heart, give me the same strength you gave Jesus in the wilderness to endure forty days of temptation. When the enemy attempts to pull me away from you and twist your words, I hold on to what I know is true about you and restore my hope in you again. In Jesus's name, amen.

DAY 216

Being a Godly Example

It is my desire to be an encouraging and challenging mentor.

As iron sharpens iron,
So a man sharpens the countenance of his friend.

—PROVERBS 27:17

Dear Lord, I thank you for the Christian sisters that have been a godly example to me throughout my life. As those relationships have been life-giving to me, I want to be a light to other women, offering a positive influence and an example of what your grace can do—a living testimony of how freedom is found in you. Give me the wisdom to counsel others without pressure to have all the answers, but to hold space for their vulnerability so they can feel seen, heard, and deeply loved. In Jesus's name, amen.

DAY 217

Jesus Satisfies My Thirst

Jesus is the living water.

Jesus answered and said to her, "Whoever drinks of this water will thirst again, but whoever drinks of the water that I shall give him will never thirst. But the water that I shall give him will become in him a fountain of water springing up into everlasting life."

—JOHN 4:13-14

Dear Jesus, you are the living water that quenches my soul. The woman at the well was rejected by society but redeemed by you. A life knowing you gives me a purpose. I am transformed and no longer thirsty for human love and validation. You know me personally and still pursue me in spite of my mistakes. In you I am free from carrying shame and you accept me, thank you. In your name I pray, amen.

DAY 218

Behold His Glory

I behold the Lord to become more like him.

But we all, with unveiled face, beholding as in a mirror the glory of the Lord, are being transformed into the same image from glory to glory, just as by the Spirit of the Lord.

—2 CORINTHIANS 3:18

Dear Father God, to behold means to fix my eyes on something remarkable. Whatever captivates my attention is who I become, so turn my eyes on your characteristics, your words, and your ways. Grow my curiosity in the Word to learn about who you are and who you say you are. Thank you for Jesus, who showed us that all we need to do is ask for help and you are right there. When I look to the Word, may I reflect your glory with each new day. In Jesus's name, amen.

DAY 219

An Obedient Heart

My obedience to God directly affects my eternal life.

He who keeps the commandment keeps his soul,
But he who is careless of his ways will die.

—PROVERBS 19:16

Dear God, I know with my mind and head that I am to obey you, but I struggle to follow through with my actions and heart. Even so, Jesus is loyal, true, and steady to me. You ask me to obey because when I walk in your ways, I'm stepping into all that you've prepared for me. When you ask me to do something, you are leading me on the best path. Give me a heart that is willing to hear your voice regarding what's best for me. In Jesus's name, amen.

DAY 220

A Resourceful Woman

Help me to be successful in all I do without fear of failure.

She considers a field and buys it;
From her profits she plants a vineyard.
She girds herself with strength,
And strengthens her arms.
She perceives that her merchandise *is* good,
And her lamp does not go out by night.

—PROVERBS 31:16-18

Dear Father God, the woman in Proverbs 31 is successful in all she does, and in her plentiful life she must be seeking you in all she does. Teach me to be a good steward of my resources. Help me to overcome my fear of failure, by entrusting the outcome of my work to you. Give me faith to manage all my work with pure intentions. In Jesus's name, amen.

DAY 221

Revival of Hearts

I pray for a revival like that of the early church.

Then those who gladly received his word were baptized;
and that day about three thousand souls were added *to them*.

—ACTS 2:41

Dear Lord, my heart longs for revival when I read about the early church. Your fearless followers boldly shared the gospel and overflowed with the power of the Holy Spirit, even in the face of persecution. I pray for many to return to you, with deep and sincere repentance of sins and a hunger to know you. May many hearts encounter you deeply and become radically transformed. In Jesus's name, amen.

DAY 222

Trusting God in Fear

I don't need to be afraid, God's got me.

In God I have put my trust;
I will not be afraid.
What can man do to me?

—PSALM 56:11

Dear God, I trust your divine protection. Like David's prayer when he was being pursued by his enemies, I am grateful to know that I can come to you when I am afraid. When I confess my fears to you, I choose you over them. Any time I'm afraid, give me confidence to face my problems because you have my back. With you by my side, I can confront them—so light my path and guide my life, especially when my troubles are daunting. In Jesus's name, amen.

DAY 223

Eternal Promises

God's Word is truth for all of eternity.

"The grass withers, the flower fades,
But the word of our God stands forever."

—ISAIAH 40:8

Dear Lord, your eternal and agape love, your joy, peace, and mercy exists for anyone who believes in Jesus. Your promises are true and can be trusted as your word reveals. You are the same yesterday, today, and tomorrow, you never fail. I'm so comforted in knowing that I am loved by a gracious Father, In Jesus's name, amen.

DAY 224

He Is Risen

Jesus rose from the dead, and it changed everything.

"He is not here; for He is risen, as He said. Come, see the place where the Lord lay. And go quickly and tell His disciples that He is risen from the dead, and indeed He is going before you into Galilee; there you will see Him. Behold, I have told you."

So they went out quickly from the tomb with fear and great joy, and ran to bring His disciples word.

—MATTHEW 28:6-8

Dear Jesus, I can only imagine the overwhelming joy your friends felt at the empty tomb. You conquered death. You were alive. This moment changed everything and proved that you're truly the Son of God. When I face anxiety or disappointment in my life, remind me that I can walk in total victory, freedom, and hope because you died for me, rose, and now live forever. In your mighty name, amen.

DAY 225

TREASURES IN HEAVEN

Waiting on his Kingdom.

"Do not lay up for yourselves treasures on earth, where moth and rust destroy and where thieves break in and steal; but lay up for yourselves treasures in heaven, where neither moth nor rust destroys and where thieves do not break in and steal."

—MATTHEW 6:19–20

Dear Father God, I wait for my circumstances to be better, when my situation will improve and be more established, when I'll be happier. I keep looking to the future and overlook where you are presently and actively moving in my life. Your words remind me that I can eagerly wait for heaven while still honoring and serving your Kingdom in my time on earth. Whether it's through spending time in prayer with you, loving on my neighbors, or serving my community; I can treasure your creation, cherish each day, and give thanks for each breath. In Jesus's name, amen.

DAY 226

Content in All Circumstances

I will learn to be content in everything.

But I rejoiced in the Lord greatly that now at last your care for me has flourished again; though you surely did care, but you lacked opportunity. Not that I speak in regard to need, for I have learned in whatever state I am, to be content: I know how to be abased, and I know how to abound. Everywhere and in all things I have learned both to be full and to be hungry, both to abound and to suffer need. I can do all things through Christ who strengthens me.

—PHILIPPIANS 4:10-13

Dear Lord, teach me what it means to be content, what it looks like to live a satisfied life not just when life is going well, but even when it feels uncertain or lacking. Like Paul writes, whether I'm in seasons of overflow and plenty or when I am in desperate need of support—may my joy and peace be rooted in you, not in what I have. When I feel restless or discouraged, remind me that you are enough and help me to rest in what I already have in you. In Jesus's name, amen.

DAY 227

Armor of God

Put the armor of God on every day.

Therefore take up the whole armor of God, that you may be able to withstand in the evil day, and having done all, to stand.
Stand therefore, having girded your waist with truth, having put on the breastplate of righteousness, and having shod your feet with the preparation of the gospel of peace; above all, taking the shield of faith with which you will be able to quench all the fiery darts of the wicked one. And take the helmet of salvation, and the sword of the Spirit, which is the word of God . . .

—EPHESIANS 6:13–17

Dear Father God, before my feet hit the floor each day, I give thanks for your armor to protect me from anything that keeps me away from you. When I'm tempted to believe lies, guard my heart, guide my thoughts, and fill me with peace so that my faith will keep me bold. When I hesitate, your word is there to be my strength, that I don't need to fight these battles alone. In Jesus's name, amen.

DAY 228

Way Maker

God makes a way where there is no way.

Your way *was* in the sea,
Your path in the great waters,
And Your footsteps were not known.
You led Your people like a flock
By the hand of Moses and Aaron.

—PSALM 77:19–20

Dear God, you parted the Red Sea for the Israelites, you saved Daniel while he was in the lion's den, and you took Joseph from prison to the palace. When I feel like I don't have enough time, strength, or faith, you remind me that you are always more than enough. You do the miraculous. You are the Way Maker, even when I can't see the way. I surrender my lack to you and lean into your abundance. In Jesus's name, amen.

DAY 229

Just Ask

Abide in him.

If you abide in Me, and My words abide in you, you will ask what you desire, and it shall be done for you.

—JOHN 15:7

Dear Jesus, sometimes I hold back from asking you for things. Maybe I doubt you, feel selfish, think it's insignificant to ask, or I forget how much you care. But you promise that if your word lives in my heart, I can be confident that whatever I ask will be heard. I don't need to worry about asking for the wrong things, because you want to hear from me. In your name, amen.

DAY 230

Sharing the Good News

We are all evangelists.

And He said to them, "Go into all the world and preach the gospel to every creature."

—MARK 16:15

Dear Jesus, it's easier to carry on about my day, to stay in my lane, but give me courage and a willing heart to share openly about my faith, about how you have transformed my life with those around me, so that their hearts may also be touched by the gospel. When I struggle to find the right things to say, you are there to give me the words. In your name I pray, amen.

DAY 231

Heart of Prayer

Prayer is never a performance.

But you, when you pray, go into your room, and when you have shut your door, pray to your Father who *is* in the secret *place*; and your Father who sees in secret will reward you openly.

—MATTHEW 6:6

Dear Jesus, I worry that my prayers don't sound good enough, especially if I don't use the right words, or sound "spiritual" enough. But that isn't what you ask of me. You made it clear that you're not looking for a polished speech or religious performance. You just want my heart. You want me to earnestly seek you as a daughter seeks her father for safety. Thank you for knowing what I need even before I speak. Help me learn to pray from a place of trust, not performance. I thank you for being my best friend. In your name, amen.

DAY 232

Godly Influence

I will influence others the way I was mentored.

Go therefore and make disciples of all the nations, baptizing them in the name of the Father and of the Son and of the Holy Spirit . . .

—MATTHEW 28:19

Dear heavenly Father, I thank you for the faithful mentors who draw me closer to you. Whether it's a family member, friend, or pastor, whether they prayed for me, spoke truth to me, or showed me warmth when I needed it, I feel you through their love. Light my way to also be a faithful disciple, and one who can encourage others to you. May my life, which has been transformed by your Spirit, point others to your infinite love and amazing grace. In Jesus's name, amen.

DAY 233

Failing Forward

Help me to keep moving forward, Lord.

For a righteous *man* may fall seven times
And rise again,
But the wicked shall fall by calamity.

—PROVERBS 24:16

Dear heavenly Father, your word says that even when I fall, I can rise again because you lift me up. You don't ask me to hide my weaknesses; you invite me to face them with you. The sooner I come to you, the more room I give your power to work through me. Your strength is made perfect in my weakness. Failure isn't the end of my journey, but it's part of my journey forward. In Jesus's name, amen.

DAY 234

Give Me Your Eyes to See Me

Help me to see myself the way you see me.

The royal daughter *is* all glorious within *the palace*;
Her clothing *is* woven with gold.

—PSALM 45:13

Dear heavenly Father, when I see myself, my flaws and shortcomings are in plain sight. You call me spotless and blameless (Ephesians 5:27). When self-doubt tells me I'm not enough, you see me as I am and still command that I can come to you no matter my state. Let me see myself through your eyes as loved and chosen. You ask me to proudly reflect your glory, and not cower behind my insecurities. In Jesus's name, amen.

DAY 235

Genuine Repentance

Repentance leads to lasting change.

"Repent therefore and be converted, that your sins may be blotted out, so that times of refreshing may come from the presence of the Lord . . ."

—ACTS 3:19

Dear heavenly Father, when I do wrong or hold on to a grudge, you want me to see sin the way you see it. I compare myself to others and feel self-righteous, but that only distances me from your transforming power. I want to be a daughter that is truly repentant of my mistakes and wrong-doings so I can turn from them wholeheartedly and experience lasting change. Please forgive my sins. In Jesus's name, amen.

DAY 236

Esteem Others

I want to honor the people around me.

Be kindly affectionate to one another with brotherly love, in honor giving preference to one another; not lagging in diligence, fervent in spirit, serving the Lord . . .

—ROMANS 12:10-11

Dear Abba Father, your word says to love and esteem others as greater than myself (Philippians 2:3), to love as you love, Lord. Help me to put the interests of others above my own, to nurture healthy relationships that reflect your loving image. Help me to share your heart with them. In Jesus's name, amen.

DAY 237

A Healthy Soul and Body

As my soul prospers, so does my health.

Beloved, I pray that you may prosper in all things and be in health, just as your soul prospers.

—3 JOHN 1:2

Dear Lord, thank you for the health you've given me, even when I have ailments. I ask you to bring my body, mind, and soul into alignment with you. Root my soul in the Word and fuel a rich prayer life so my outward physical state can reflect my inward spiritual growth. You entrusted me with life; may I honor it with healthy habits that nourish my physical body, guard my mind with truth, and fill my heart with gratitude. Please give me peace and rehabilitation. Remove and mend anything that keeps me from honoring the life you've gifted me. In Jesus's name, amen.

DAY 238

Pursue Peace

God's peace is better than worldly conflict.

The beginning of strife *is like* releasing water;
Therefore stop contention before a quarrel starts.

—PROVERBS 17:14

Dear God, conflict is an inevitable part of life, and I am imperfect in relationship with other imperfect people. When I disagree with someone, I tend to want things to go my way and insist on being understood rather than seeking to understand. When I am in a struggle, grow my belief to trust that everything is in your hands. Give me the wisdom to respond with love and grace and the strength and humility to pursue peace from the Holy Spirit. In Jesus's name, amen.

DAY 239

Matchless Glory

Magnify the Lord; seek the Lord.

Oh, magnify the LORD with me,
And let us exalt His name together.

—PSALM 34:3

Heavenly Father, as the King of Kings and Lord of Lords, you are matchless in majesty. With my every breath, I sing and shout your praises. I want to seize each opportunity to give you thanks for everything you've done in my life, whether it's to testify of your faithfulness, a healed wound, accompanying me in my painful moments, or a miraculous breakthrough. You deserve all the credit. Even when I'm in a valley, I want to declare that you are faithful and good. In Jesus's name, amen.

DAY 240

Revival of Nations

I pray for revival across this world.

If My people who are called by My name will humble themselves, and pray and seek My face, and turn from their wicked ways, then I will hear from heaven, and will forgive their sin and heal their land.

—2 CHRONICLES 7:14

Dear heavenly Jesus, my heart aches for those who are lost and in need of healing because I, too, am among them. Many of us try to make sense of our identity and purpose because we don't know or forget that God created us intentionally with love. I pray we clearly see and feel the joy and freedom that comes from knowing you. May revival grow, beginning with one heart at a time. In your name, amen.

DAY 241

Faith then Works

To have faith is to believe.

But someone will say, "You have faith, and I have works." Show me your faith without your works, and I will show you my faith by my works. You believe that there is one God. You do well. Even the demons believe—and tremble!

—JAMES 2:18-19

Dear Jesus, true faith flows from experiencing your love firsthand. I seek to live out what I believe, not just in what I say but how I interact with and serve others. If my actions don't match what I believe, please reveal the disconnect and fortify my faith. When I fall short, remind me I don't stand condemned, because you have already secured my place in heaven. In your name, amen.

DAY 242

Healing Health

Healing is possible, with God.

Behold, I will bring it health and healing; I will heal them and reveal to them the abundance of peace and truth.

—JEREMIAH 33:6

Dear Lord, I pray for your healing over any part of my body that isn't functioning as you designed it. Touch every part that's hurting with your healing hand and make it well. Healing may not come in my desired time frame or in the way I expect, but I want to trust that your way is perfect. Even if I receive unexpected or disappointing news, I trust you and those who are entrusted to care for me. Remind me that beyond our physical bodies, it is wholeness, with you, on the inside that I seek. Thank you for healing every part of me. In Jesus's name, amen.

DAY 243

Thankful for Being Saved

I give God thanks for everything.

I will praise the name of God with a song,
And will magnify Him with thanksgiving.

—PSALM 69:30

Dear God, I am so thankful for you, for how you love me. Your word says you leave the ninety-nine to save the one (Matthew 18:12). You save me when I wander and you rescue me, carrying me back when I'm too weak and worn. I pray for a heart bent toward thankfulness, regardless of my circumstances, because you're always with me and your love for me never changes. In Jesus's name, amen.

DAY 244

Walk Uprightly

May my walk reflect your character.

I know also, my God, that You test the heart and have pleasure in uprightness. As for me, in the uprightness of my heart I have willingly offered all these *things*; and now with joy I have seen Your people, who are present here to offer willingly to You.

—1 CHRONICLES 29:17

Dear Father God, you call me to live differently from the world, not to appear better than others but because I love you and want to honor you. Give me the courage to walk with a sincere heart and without self-serving motives in all I do. Keep me on your path so that my walk reflects your character. Let your light shine through my words, actions, and perspectives so that others can experience your goodness. In Jesus's name, amen.

DAY 245

Pure Hearts See God

Having a pure heart brings me closer to the Lord.

Blessed *are* the pure in heart,
For they shall see God.

—MATTHEW 5:8

Dear God, bless me with a pure heart like Jesus, one that is sincere and humble. He was never hypocritical, never envious, and his actions were motivated by his deep love for you. When my heart begins to wander or deceive me, clear the pride, fear, and confusion and direct me back to you. I want to be a witness to your hand at work in every part of my life. In Jesus's name, amen.

DAY 246

All In

Give me an undivided heart.

Trust in the LORD with all your heart,
And lean not on your own understanding . . .

—PROVERBS 3:5

Dear Father God, you ask me to be all in, not one foot in my ways and one in yours, but fully surrendered. You desire my love not just intellectually, but emotionally and spiritually. Give me an undivided heart, loyal only to you. I don't want to offer you my scraps or leftovers, I want to give you my best. As Mary broke her alabaster jar and poured out costly perfume at Jesus's feet, I pour out my life before you. Take all of me, Lord. In Jesus's name, amen.

DAY 247

He Has Overcome the World

I will face tribulations in this life, but my God has already overcome them.

"These things I have spoken to you, that in Me you may have peace. In the world you will have tribulation; but be of good cheer, I have overcome the world."

—JOHN 16:33

Dear Lord, you remind me that I don't need to fear when circumstances beyond my control arise or when life tests my capacity and limits. You are already on the other side of each trial I face. You go before me, walk beside me, and guard from behind me. Nothing catches you by surprise. Even when I experience heartbreak, grief, and sorrow, you've already told us how everything ends, with the return of Jesus. Help me not to doubt your goodness when I'm facing trials. In Jesus's name, amen.

DAY 248

True Identity

My identity is now found in Jesus.

For our citizenship is in heaven, from which we also eagerly wait for the Savior, the Lord Jesus Christ, who will transform our lowly body that it may be conformed to His glorious body, according to the working by which He is able even to subdue all things to Himself.

—PHILIPPIANS 3:20–21

Dear heavenly Father, thank you for giving me an identity in you! In you I know exactly who I am—I am accepted as your child. I don't need to worry about where I belong or where home is. I bring every broken piece of my life to you, unafraid that you'll reject me. Society labels me by what I have, what I've done, or what I look like, but you say I'm chosen and loved. Help me take off every false identity I've worn and instead clothe me in the truth of who I am: a child of God. In Jesus's name, amen.

DAY 249

Hope in God

Why be disappointed when I am so blessed?

Why are you cast down, O my soul?
And why are you disquieted within me?
Hope in God;
For I shall yet praise Him,
The help of my countenance and my God.

—PSALM 42:11

Lord Jesus, I can feel shame for feeling disappointment when I know I am blessed. But I bring it to you today because you see it and comfort me. Thank you for loving me even when I am ungrateful, frustrated, and tired. You not only give my life blessings, you *are* the blessing. Steady my heart to trust you. In your name I pray, amen.

DAY 250

Obeying God, Not Man

I want to put God's will over the will of other people.

And He would not allow anyone to carry wares through the temple. Then He taught, saying to them, "Is it not written, 'My house shall be called a house of prayer for all nations'? But you have made it a 'den of thieves.'"

—MARK 11:16-17

Dear Jesus, you fiercely defend and protect the place of prayer as a place that is open to all. I'm reminded that I can be led by rules and transactions to earn your love; that only gets in the way of being in relationship with you. Humble me and give me the desire to come to you in worship, receive the gift of fellowship with other believers, and be wholly satisfied in being personally connected in your presence. In your name, amen.

DAY 251

The Weight of Perfectionism

Jesus is perfect, so I don't need to be.

"[He] committed no sin,
Nor was deceit found in His mouth" . . .

—1 PETER 2:22

Dear heavenly Father, Jesus lived a perfect, sinless life on earth, and as hard as I may try, I know I never will achieve it. I often feel the pressure to be perfect at work, at home, and even at church. I compare myself with others, strive to perform, and end up worn down. Please free me from the weight of perfectionism and the pressure to look like I have it all together. Teach me to rely on your strength when I fall short. In Jesus's name, amen.

DAY 252

Open Arms

God's arms are always open.

"And the son said to him, 'Father, I have sinned against heaven and in your sight, and am no longer worthy to be called your son.'
"But the father said to his servants, 'Bring out the best robe and put *it* on him, and put a ring on his hand and sandals on *his* feet. And bring the fatted calf here and kill *it*, and let us eat and be merry; for this my son was dead and is alive again; he was lost and is found.' And they began to be merry."

—LUKE 15:21–24

Dear heavenly Father, Jesus teaches the parable of the prodigal son to reveal lessons about your love. Like the prodigal son, my pride makes me believe that trusting myself is somehow better than trusting you. But Jesus shares that you remain faithful to me, waiting and celebrating my return without asking for anything in return, regardless of whether I am deserving of that deep love. Humble me so I can confess freely and return to you. And like the father, who doesn't withhold love from personal resentments, anger, or hurt, your love is so much deeper and always flowing. Thank you for being faithful to me. In Jesus's name, amen.

DAY 253

Serve One Master

I want to be influenced by God, not the world.

"No one can serve two masters; for either he will hate the one and love the other, or else he will be loyal to the one and despise the other. You cannot serve God and mammon."

—MATTHEW 6:24

Dear God, the world is constantly telling me I need stuff to be happy, whether it's from social media or the influence of my peers. I can easily fall prey to materialism, feeling entitled to certain possessions or a status level, ultimately accumulating what will never satisfy my soul. You remind me that we can choose to live differently, and that we are set apart, just as Jesus was. Show me how to be content with my circumstances, reveal where I value my time. Give me wisdom for decision-making and how I spend my resources, so that I may repent and receive your forgiveness. In Jesus's name, amen.

DAY 254

Self-Sacrificial Love

I want to put others before myself.

Let nothing *be done* through selfish ambition or conceit, but in lowliness of mind let each esteem others better than himself.

—PHILIPPIANS 2:3

Dear Lord, thank you for loving me and shaping me to become more like Jesus. Uproot the parts of me that still cling to comfort over obedience. Work in my heart to reflect yours so I can love others freely. When I have a choice between what's easy and what's right, I want to choose what honors you. In Jesus's name, amen.

DAY 255

A Woman Who Loves the Lord

People will praise the woman I am because of the Lord.

Her children rise up and call her blessed;
Her husband *also*, and he praises her:
"Many daughters have done well,
But you excel them all."
Charm *is* deceitful and beauty *is* passing,
But a woman *who* fears the LORD, she shall be praised.
Give her of the fruit of her hands,
And let her own works praise her in the gates.

—PROVERBS 31:28-31

Dear God, I pray my character reflects your heart—a heart rooted in Jesus and shaped by your word. Build up my worth and cultivate a character that lasts, one of humility and love for you. Charm and beauty may catch people's eyes for a moment, but I want to live the joy of a fruitful life that comes from walking closely with you. In Jesus's name, amen.

DAY 256

Give Me Eyes to See You

God is always moving, even when I don't recognize it.

So it was, while they conversed and reasoned, that Jesus Himself drew near and went with them. But their eyes were restrained, so that they did not know Him.

—LUKE 24:15-16

Dear Jesus, like the disciples who didn't recognize you after your resurrection, there are times when I don't realize you're with me. Remind me when you show up in a way I don't expect, that you may be moving in a way I don't yet recognize. In your wonderful name, amen.

DAY 257

Worthy of Worship

The Lord is always worthy of worship and praise.

Exalt the LORD our God,
And worship at His footstool—
He *is* holy.

—PSALM 99:5

Dear Lord, I'm in awe of who you are. You spoke the heavens and earth into existence. When I think about your greatness, the depth of your love, and all you've done, I'm left in amazement and wonder. You are holy and worthy of all my praise. There is no flaw in you. You never change. Most wonderful of all, you gave me Jesus. In Jesus's name, amen.

DAY 258

Obey the Last Thing

His instruction is the way forward.

Then He said to them, "Take heed what you hear. With the same measure you use, it will be measured to you; and to you who hear, more will be given. For whoever has, to him more will be given; but whoever does not have, even what he has will be taken away from him."

—MARK 4:24–25

Dear Jesus, I confess that I'm often looking for an answer without fully following through on something you may have already revealed. But the truth is that my obedience to your last instruction can be a clue to receiving what you want to show me next. Help me to truly hear what you want me to hear and not just the parts I want to hear. In your precious name, amen.

DAY 259

Hearing God's Voice

God is always speaking.

My sheep hear My voice, and I know them, and they follow Me.

—JOHN 10:27

Dear heavenly Father, as your daughter, I want to recognize your voice and trust it above all others. So many voices compete for my attention. Your voice is quiet but always near, always pursuing me even when I am distracted. Please guide me to the quiet place with you so that I can discern you speaking into my life. I want to follow your gentle guidance with no hesitation, just as sheep faithfully follow their shepherd. In Jesus's name, amen.

DAY 260

Cast Your Cares

The Lord is trustworthy; I can cast my anxiety on him.

Consider the ravens, for they neither sow nor reap, which have neither storehouse nor barn; and God feels them. Of how much more value are you than the birds?

LUKE 12:24

Dear God, you're the God who holds the universe in your hands, and yet, you care about every detail of my life—big and small. You meet the needs of lilies and sparrows. How much more you must love and care for me! I surrender all my cares and anxiety onto you because you love me and know what's truly best for me. I give you everything that's weighing on my heart and causing my worries. In Jesus's name, amen.

DAY 261

BUILT TO STAND

The Lord holds me up.

"Therefore whoever hears these sayings of Mine, and does them, I will liken him to a wise man who built his house on the rock: and the rain descended, the floods came, and the winds blew and beat on that house; and it did not fall, for it was founded on the rock . . ."

—MATTHEW 7:24-25

Dear Father God, when my life gets shaken up and feels unstable, I'm reminded of what truly matters. You are the solid foundation I've built my life upon. When the rain descends, floodwaters rise, and winds knock against me, I don't need to panic or stress about anything because my hope is anchored in what's eternal. My relationship with you is the solid ground I stand on. Remind me when everything shifts that I can rest on you as my steady rock. In Jesus's name, amen.

DAY 262

DEEP RELATIONSHIPS

Relationships can be restored, with the help of the Lord.

And be kind to one another, tenderhearted, forgiving one another, even as God in Christ forgave you.

—EPHESIANS 4:32

Dear Lord, thank you for the friendships you've put in my life. Some have stayed many years, and others only for a season, but I know you've used each one to grow me. Guide me to pursue deep connections, ones that foster enriching and healthy relationships and draw me closer to you. Like Jesus, make me a loyal, loving friend who encourages others in their walk with you. When conflict and misunderstandings arise, don't let offense take root in my heart and give me the kindness to be quick to forgive. In Jesus's name, amen.

DAY 263

Freedom from Condemnation

Conviction is from God; condemnation is from the enemy.

There is therefore now no condemnation to those who are in Christ Jesus, who do not walk according to the flesh, but according to the Spirit.

—ROMANS 8:1

Dear Lord, when I hear an accusing voice that questions my worth and your love for me, help me recognize it for what it is: just a lie trying to make me forget who I am in you. The truth is, because of Jesus and his work on the cross, I'm no longer under condemnation. You're not a stern, unloving, and distant father who's waiting to chastise me for messing up; instead, you draw me into your loving and gracious arms. In Jesus's name, amen.

DAY 264

Gather Around

We were meant to live life with others.

Now all who believed were together, and had all things in common, and sold their possessions and goods, and divided them among all, as anyone had need.
So continuing daily with one accord in the temple, and breaking bread from house to house, they ate their food with gladness and simplicity of heart . . .

—ACTS 2:44–46

Dear God, thank you for the community of believers, family, and friends that surround me. I'm grateful for the gift of gathering over shared meals and honest conversations that remind me we are not alone. When life gets overwhelming, it can be easy to isolate from others. Help me to lean on those you have placed in my life and to see your reflection in them. In Jesus's name, amen.

DAY 265

Don't Trust in Riches

I don't want to be easily influenced to live outside of my means.

Therefore humble yourselves under the mighty hand of God, that He may exalt you in due time, casting all your care upon Him, for He cares for you.

— 1 PETER 5:6-7

Dear Lord, you see me when I am afraid and worried about my security, but let me rest in your provision rather than the balance in my bank. Expand my vision so that I remember you take care of me and the true riches in my life are spiritual blessings of your love and grace. I know you will provide for me through every season. In Jesus's name, amen.

DAY 266

Save My Loved Ones

I trust the Lord for the salvation of my family.

So they said, "Believe on the Lord Jesus Christ, and you will be saved, you and your household."

—ACTS 16:31

Dear heavenly Father, my heart aches for the people I love who don't know you or have walked away from you. I long for them to experience your unconditional love, forgiveness, and kindness. It's difficult to see their hearts far from you, but I know they are not beyond your reach and you patiently watch over them. Bring them comfort and healing of the rift that led to their distance. Their salvation is in your hands and I commit to praying for them to turn to you, so that they may come to know and love you deeply. Soften their hearts and open their eyes so they can no longer ignore you. In Jesus's name, amen.

DAY 267

Redeeming My Time

I want to make the best use of the time I am given.

See then that you walk circumspectly, not as fools but as wise, redeeming the time, because the days are evil.

—EPHESIANS 5:15-16

Dear heavenly Father, thank you for the gift of time. Guide me to be more intentional about how I spend my time and to prioritize ways I can deepen my connection with you. Instead of falling prey to the traps that steal my time, I want to focus on seeking your presence and voice, accompanying my walk in life on the path you've set before me. In Jesus's name, amen.

DAY 268

My Loved Ones' Safety

I trust the Lord with the safety of my family.

The LORD *is* your keeper;
The LORD *is* your shade at your right hand.
The sun shall not strike you by day,
Nor the moon by night.

The LORD shall preserve you from all evil;
He shall preserve your soul.
The LORD shall preserve your going out and your coming in,
From this time forth, and even forevermore.

—PSALM 121:5-8

Dear God, please watch over my loved ones. Guard their going out and their coming in, during daylight and darkness, and in unexpected storms. Provide for them the protection, wisdom, strength, and peace they need as they navigate their way. Keep them, bless them, and let them know you are with them wherever they are. In Jesus's name, amen.

DAY 269

Losing Someone Dear

God is my comforter when I am sad.

Blessed *are* those who mourn,
For they shall be comforted.

—MATTHEW 5:4

Dear Jesus, today I come to you with a broken heart. I'm flooded with overwhelming loss, grief, and heartache. It's unbearable to sit with the pain of losing someone dear to me, someone I've deeply loved, and knowing I can't experience their loving presence again in this lifetime fills me with an inconsolable sorrow. I wish I could tell them how grateful I am for their love and for the ways they've made my life richer and fuller, how I felt your love flowing through them. In this sadness, only you can meet me in the exact coordinates of my pain. You weep with me because you loved them and grieve their loss with me. You hold me close and dry my eyes. In your name I pray, amen.

DAY 270

Being Poured Into

I desire for mentors in my life to encourage growth and maturity in Christ.

Listen to counsel and receive instruction,
That you may be wise in your latter days.

—PROVERBS 19:20

Dear God, I desire to have faithful mentors to walk alongside me and pour into me. You didn't create me to walk through life alone, but to be encouraged and to encourage others as we do life together. Keep me humble and open to loving correction, and send me the right counselors for this season of my life. Give me wisdom to receive what's from you, and guard my heart from idolizing them or putting any person on a pedestal. In Jesus's name, amen.

DAY 271

Purpose in Pruning

Pruning is refining.

"I am the true vine, and My Father is the vinedresser. Every branch in Me that does not bear fruit He takes away; and every *branch* that bears fruit He prunes, that it may bear more fruit. You are already clean because of the word which I have spoken to you."

—JOHN 15:1-3

Dear God, when my weaknesses rise to the surface, it's not to condemn me but to set me free. I release what you're pruning away, including any habits that no longer serve your purpose in me. Even when it might hurt to let go, remind me you're doing it because you see the fruit that's yet to come. I am your work of art. I trust you're making room for buds of growth that are more aligned to who you've called me to be. In Jesus's name, amen.

DAY 272

Eternal Joy

When breakthrough comes, so does joy and honor.

Instead of your shame *you shall have* double *honor,*
And *instead of* confusion they shall rejoice in their portion.
Therefore in their land they shall possess double;
Everlasting joy shall be theirs.

—ISAIAH 61:7

Dear Father, keep your word in my heart, transform my shame into honor and my confusion into joy and peace. I carry on my heart the weight of my shortcomings. Whether it's from my past failures or wounds from others—I bring it to you today! And you remind me of my inheritance and replace this heaviness with everlasting joy. I am light because you choose and restore me. Thank you. In Jesus's name, amen.

DAY 273

Clean Heart

I experience renewal in Christ.

Create in me a clean heart, O God,
And renew a steadfast spirit within me.
Do not cast me away from Your presence,
And do not take Your Holy Spirit from me.

—PSALM 51:10–11

Dear Lord, refresh my spirit, purify me from sin, guilt, heaviness. Give me a new heart that is ready to follow you. Help me to walk in step with the Holy Spirit and thank you for your grace when I get it wrong. When I stumble, and my heart feels cluttered and far from you, may I come before you and release it to you. Teach me to bring it to you without any hesitation. Give me a willing heart, and a hope to remember the pure joy I can experience when I am wholly surrendered to your love. In Jesus's name, amen.

DAY 274

Delight in Truth

I am a delight to the Lord when I am honest in all things.

Lying lips *are* an abomination to the LORD,
But those who deal truthfully *are* His delight.

—PROVERBS 12:22

Dear Father God, being deceitful doesn't always look like the obvious sneaky or malicious acts that we think of. But being deceitful in everyday life might take on seemingly benign or harmless forms like trying to appear virtuous to others, bending or withholding the truth, avoiding facing a truth out of comfort, or being performative in faith—all of which encourage my heart to hide in shadows and hinder me from becoming the daughter you've created me to be. You're a God of truth, and you delight in me walking in truth. Help me speak always with a pure heart and clean tongue, even when it isn't easy. In Jesus's name, amen.

DAY 275

Sharing God's Message

His flawless vision for his people.

But as we have been approved by God to be entrusted with the gospel, even so we speak, not as pleasing men, but God who tests our hearts.

—1 THESSALONIANS 2:4

Dear Lord, when you give me a revelation from your word, it's not so that I can become puffed up in my knowledge with pride, but to give you all the glory. Any vision you give your people is not for personal gain, but about your larger plan to proclaim what Jesus did. Thank you for using me as a vessel so others can see that every promise in your word will come to pass. May my words always reflect your goodness. In Jesus's name, amen.

DAY 276

Humbled by Grace

I want to be like the tax collector, not the Pharisee.

"The Pharisee stood and prayed thus with himself, 'God, I thank You that I am not like other men—extortioners, unjust, adulterers, or even as this tax collector. I fast twice a week; I give tithes of all that I possess.' And the tax collector, standing afar off, would not so much as raise *his* eyes to heaven, but beat his breast, saying, 'God, be merciful to me a sinner!' I tell you, this man went down to his house justified *rather* than the other; for everyone who exalts himself will be humbled, and he who humbles himself will be exalted."

—LUKE 18:11-14

Dear heavenly Father, we could have the fanciest titles and fame on earth, but it doesn't matter if my heart isn't right before you. I need your grace. Keep me from being deceived into the belief that my efforts will gain your love. Thank you for your saving grace, which is a free gift, with no strings attached. Thank you for sending Jesus to die on the cross for my sins to make me worthy of that mercy. In Jesus's name, amen.

DAY 277

Seeking Your Will

I want God's will, not mine.

I can of Myself do nothing. As I hear, I judge; and My judgment is righteous, because I do not seek My own will but the will of the Father who sent Me.

—JOHN 5:30

Dear Jesus, you show us what it means to live with a completely surrendered heart that seeks the will of the Father. There are times when I begin to pray and I already have an idea of what I want to happen, and it blocks me from being open to God's voice. Prime my heart to follow you and reveal to me where my will is a roadblock to letting God work in me! In your precious name, amen.

DAY 278

Fruitful in Spirit and Actions

I want to be fruitful in my faith.

And seeing from afar a fig tree having leaves, He went to see if perhaps He would find something on it. When He came to it, He found nothing but leaves, for it was not the season for figs. In response Jesus said to it, "Let no one eat fruit from you ever again."
And His disciples heard *it*.

—MARK 11:13–14

Dear Father, when you speak, mountains move, birds sing. When Jesus cursed the fig tree, he demonstrated a powerful lesson to his disciples—the importance of being fruitful through our actions and in our spiritual lives. Show me what spiritual fruitfulness looks like in my life. How can I be a faithful daughter to you in both my actions and heart? Please stir my heart and shape my thoughts. In Jesus's name, amen.

DAY 279

Purpose in Christ

I have been created to do the work of my Father in heaven.

I planted, Apollos watered, but God gave the increase. So then neither he who plants is anything, nor he who waters, but God who gives the increase. Now he who plants and he who waters are one, and each one will receive his own reward according to his own labor.

For we are God's fellow workers; you are God's field, *you are* God's building. According to the grace of God which was given to me, as a wise master builder I have laid the foundation, and another builds on it. But let each one take heed how he builds on it. For no other foundation can anyone lay than that which is laid, which is Jesus Christ.

—1 CORINTHIANS 3:6-11

Dear Lord, you have created me for this exact moment in history to be a partner in the work you've prepared in advance for me. Whether you call me to have a conversation with a neighbor, or cook a meal for a sick friend, root me in the only perfect foundation: Jesus. Remind me that the increase comes from you alone; my job is to care for and nurture the gifts you've entrusted to me and trust you with the results of my actions. Give me boldness to serve you and step into each divine assignment you have for me each day. In Jesus's name, amen.

DAY 280

FREE FROM NEEDING MORE

To be content with the "minimum" is the goal.

> Now godliness with contentment is great gain. For we brought nothing into *this* world, *and it is* certain we can carry nothing out. And having food and clothing, with these we shall be content.
>
> —1 TIMOTHY 6:6-8

Dear God—I confess I always need "something more." I believe lies that whisper that I don't have enough and that you aren't enough. I want to experience fulfillment with where you've placed me. Empower me to refuse the restless search for satisfaction outside of you; all I need to do is see that everything I already have and need is in you. In Jesus's name, amen.

DAY 281

KEEP ME HONEST

Honesty leads to eternal life.

> "God *is* Spirit, and those who worship Him must worship in spirit and truth."
>
> —JOHN 4:24

Dear Father God, you wish to see my heart's true state. When I confess my hardships and trials, through prayer, journaling, praise, or when I lift up my grief to you, you say that confession is an act of worship. You delight in my bare honesty, even when you already know and delight when I bring it to you. You urge us to pursue an authentic relationship with you and others. Keep me honest and vulnerable because I can trust in you. In Jesus's name, amen.

DAY 282

Called Out of Darkness

I have been called out of darkness; I am chosen.

But you *are* a chosen generation, a royal priesthood, a holy nation, His own special people, that you may proclaim the praises of Him who called you out of darkness into His marvelous light . . .

—1 PETER 2:9

Dear heavenly Father, I thank you for calling me out of darkness and choosing me as your own. I'm a daughter of the King and yet, I often forget that truth. It's easy to see myself as flawed or ordinary, but you see me through the lens of grace, made whole by Jesus. Remind me daily of who I am in you. I will praise you forever, not because of what I've done, but because of who you are. In Jesus's name, amen.

DAY 283

Honesty Is the Best Policy

May I walk in integrity.

Do not lie to one another, since you have put off the old man with his deeds, and have put on the new *man* who is renewed in knowledge according to the image of Him who created him . . .

—COLOSSIANS 3:9–10

Dear Lord, sometimes being honest means I risk looking weak, admit to failure, or am seen in a negative light. When I'm dishonest, you see what's lying at the bottom of my heart, my anxiety and worries about not getting life right or insecurity about making the wrong choices. You see my bare self as I am, and simply ask me to turn toward you. Father, I confess for the times I act or speak in ways that I'm not proud of. Give me clear eyes and heart, to hold myself accountable and to move through my days with integrity. Just as Jesus bravely uplifted the rejected and outcasts, give me the courage to stand in honesty and seek your face. In Jesus's name, amen.

DAY 284

Beauty of God

Let the beauty of God's favor shine on me.

And let the beauty of the LORD our God be upon us,
And establish the work of our hands for us;
Yes, establish the work of our hands.

—PSALM 90:17

Dear God, you have empowered us to fulfill our calling with you by our side, with gifts of talents and strengths. Just as you equipped Bezalel and Aholiab with the creativity, skills, labor, and knowledge to construct the Tabernacle (Exodus 31:1–6), you establish the work of my hands so they can be an offering to worship and lift you up. Let your favor rest on me as I labor for your glory. In Jesus's name, amen.

DAY 285

Praying for Others

When I pray for others, I am doing the work of the Lord.

For this reason we also, since the day we heard it, do not cease to pray for you, and to ask that you may be filled with the knowledge of His will in all wisdom and spiritual understanding . . .

—COLOSSIANS 1:9

Dear heavenly Father, grow in my heart a desire and generosity to regularly pray for others in my life, with sincerity and persistence for those you've placed on my heart. Use me to intercede on their behalf, just as Jesus faithfully intercedes for me. Show me practical ways I can encourage and lift them up, so they know they're not alone and you are drawing them near. Thank you for working through me and designating me to be a vessel of your love and grace to bless others. In Jesus's name, amen.

DAY 286

Daily Bread

He is our provider.

In this manner, therefore, pray:

Our Father in heaven,
Hallowed be Your name.
Your kingdom come.
Your will be done
On earth as *it is* in heaven.
Give us this day our daily bread.

—MATTHEW 6:9–11

Dear Father God, you always provide what I need, exactly when I need it. Sometimes it feels like it's not enough and I demand to know why certain prayers go unanswered, but when I come back to the daily bread, you are asking me to trust that you will give me what I need in each moment, even when I don't know how you will provide. May I turn to these comforting words as a reminder that I can always come to the Lord's Prayer whenever I am lost and don't know how to start my prayer. It is in this simple and powerful prayer that you tell me that you are the One who provides the daily nourishment each day to sustain me both physically and spiritually. Thank you, Lord, for my daily bread. In Jesus's name, amen.

DAY 287

RICH IN WISDOM

Show me the wise path in life.

How much better to get wisdom than gold! And to get understanding is to be chosen rather than silver.

—PROVERBS 16:16

Dear Lord, nothing in this world is hidden from you. You can never mislead me or steer me wrong, you always show me the wisest path. When you allow challenges in my life, you're increasing my wisdom and helping me grow. You know what I need today and what I'll need tomorrow, and you equip me to walk in victory. In Jesus's name, amen.

DAY 288

THE PROMISE OF SORROW'S END

Though I may be sad now, it will not last forever.

"And God will wipe away every tear from their eyes; there shall be no more death, nor sorrow, nor crying. There shall be no more pain, for the former things have passed away."

—REVELATION 21:4

Dear Abba Father, eternity with you holds wholeness, comfort, and restoration. You comfort me and gently wipe my tears when I bring my sorrow and heartbreak to you. Thank you for covering me with your wings. You give us a clear picture of what we can expect when we meet you in heaven. You will erase my grief, and in your presence, suffering will be replaced with a joy and perfect confidence in your Kingdom. In Jesus's name, amen.

DAY 289

Deliverer

God fights my battles for me.

" 'For the Lord your God *is* He who goes with you, to fight for you against your enemies, to save you.' "

—DEUTERONOMY 20:4

Dear heavenly Father, just as you delivered the Israelites from Pharaoh's army at the Red Sea, you make a way when there seems to be none. You save me from what I cannot escape on my own. Thank you for fighting for me and defending me better than I ever could. Even when you don't remove the battle, you equip me to stand firm, in your armor and armed with the sword of your word. Thank you for providing a way out of temptation. In Jesus's name, amen.

DAY 290

Taking Thoughts Captive

Every thought has to bow at the name of Jesus.

For the weapons of our warfare *are* not carnal but mighty in God for pulling down strongholds, casting down arguments and every high thing that exalts itself against the knowledge of God, bringing every thought into captivity to the obedience of Christ, and being ready to punish all disobedience when your obedience is fulfilled.

—2 CORINTHIANS 10:4-6

Dear Lord, my mind can feel like a battlefield. Overthinking makes me doubt my worth, question my purpose, or wonder where I belong. The enemy knows how to twist my thoughts, but you give me the power to fight back with truth. Forgive me for believing lies that weren't from you, for believing I'm too flawed to be used for your glory. I want to bring every thought captive into the light of your truth. Align my thoughts with your truth. In Jesus's name, amen.

DAY 291

Perfect Love

God's love drowns out fear.

There is no fear in love; but perfect love casts out fear, because fear involves torment. But he who fears has not been made perfect in love.

—1 JOHN 4:18

Dear heavenly Father, I confess that fear hinders me from experiencing your love. I can get caught up in every "what-if" scenario and start building walls to protect myself. When fear rises like a tide, draw me into the deeper waters of your perfect love, which drowns out all fear. In your love, I'm fully known and fully safe with you. When I start to worry, remind me that the One who loves me is also the one who holds my future. In Jesus's name, amen.

DAY 292

Persevering in Doing Good

I want to persevere in doing good, even if the world and people around me are not.

And let us not grow weary while doing good, for in due season we shall reap if we do not lose heart.

—GALATIANS 6:9

Dear Father, even when I strive to do good, I don't always make the right choices. Especially when I see others taking shortcuts and thriving. But you tell us true reward comes from being faithful to you. Teach me to stay the course and keep living according to your ways, to honor you even when no one notices, or when it goes unrewarded. In Jesus's name, amen.

DAY 293

Intentional Fellowship

I want to be intentional with the people you've placed in my life.

And let us consider one another in order to stir up love and good works, not forsaking the assembling of ourselves together, as *is* the manner of some, but exhorting *one another*, and so much the more as you see the Day approaching.

—HEBREWS 10:24-25

Dear God, thank you for the wise counsel of believers you've brought into my sphere of connections—to share life with, share struggles and triumphs, and most importantly, to glorify you with. I want to be intentional with those you have placed in my life. Help us to stir one another to do good works in love. Help me serve the body of believers I'm in and guide me to be intentional in my relationships with the people you have placed in my life. In Jesus's name, amen.

DAY 294

Success with God

If I put God first, there's no way not to be successful.

This Book of the Law shall not depart from your mouth, but you shall meditate in it day and night, that you may observe to do according to all that is written in it. For then you will make your way prosperous, and then you will have good success.

—JOSHUA 1:8

Dear God, I don't want success apart from you. The world defines success by wealth, status, and applause, but true success is found in obedience and trust in you. If I gain everything in this world, but my soul is prideful, life is meaningless. Help me to pursue meaning through you, to bear lasting fruit. In Jesus's name, amen.

DAY 295

Abundant Life in Christ

The promise of a purpose driven life.

The thief does not come except to steal, and to kill, and to destroy. I have come that they may have life, and that they may have *it* more abundantly.

—JOHN 10:10

Dear Lord Jesus, you want more for me in my life than what I often settle for. You offer me a life that is full of meaning and joy, not one to be lived out of survival. The enemy tries to rob me of a life blessed by you by distracting, draining, and deceiving me from being connected to you. I give thanks because you were sent to the world for me and because of that, I'm safe in the tender love and care of my Shepherd. In your name, amen.

DAY 296

Fully Forgiven

Receive God's forgiveness.

As far as the east is from the west,
So far has He removed our transgressions from us.

—PSALM 103:12

Dear heavenly Father, thank you for your unwavering love. Sometimes it's hard to fully grasp that you've truly forgiven me and that you don't hold any of my sins against me. I find myself replaying my past mistakes even though you've removed them. You accept me as completely clean and treat me as if I've never sinned. Release any guilt that no longer belongs to me, so I can fully believe and receive your forgiveness with my whole heart. In Jesus's name, amen.

DAY 297

Relinquishing Control

I am giving up control, knowing God has my future in his hands.

For I know the thoughts that I think toward you, says the Lord, thoughts of peace and not of evil, to give you a future and a hope.

—JEREMIAH 29:11

Dear Lord, you know I like to be in control. You know that I even have the audacity to give you, the sovereign King of the Universe, suggestions. When I spiral into overthinking, give me the courage to surrender how I want things to go, and trust you to know what's best. Your plans are always good and go beyond what I can expect. Everything you allow is within your provision. In Jesus's name, amen.

DAY 298

Faithful Stewardship

The work of my hands will produce a harvest.

He who tills his land will be satisfied with bread,
But he who follows frivolity *is* devoid of understanding.

—PROVERBS 12:11

"His lord said to him, 'Well *done*, good and faithful servant; you were faithful over a few things, I will make you ruler over many things. Enter into the joy of your lord.'"

—MATTHEW 25:21

Dear heavenly Father, you've entrusted me to be a faithful steward of the time, talents, and treasures you've given me. Give me a work ethic that honors you. Open my eyes so I see opportunities to serve, love, and minister. I know there's a rich satisfaction in building discipline and seeing the fruits of my efforts. But ultimately, I know it will all be worth it when I hear from you "Well done, my good and faithful servant." In Jesus's name, amen.

DAY 299

Yielding My Heart

I pray God aligns my desires with his purposes.

"Father, if it is Your will, take this cup away from Me; nevertheless not My will, but Yours, be done."

—LUKE 22:42

Dear Lord, you never see my needs and hopes as a hindrance to your ultimate plan. When I come to you with my earnest desires, you see my true heart. Help me to recognize the gifts you've granted and uniquely placed in me. In whatever I pursue to use these gifts, give me wisdom and guidance to ultimately serve your purpose. Grow my belief in you so I can hear your voice in my life. In Jesus's name, amen.

DAY 300

Keeping Your Word

I want to be a woman of my word.

"But let your 'Yes' be 'Yes,' and your 'No,' 'No.' For whatever is more than these is from the evil one."

—MATTHEW 5:37

Dear Lord, I want to be a woman of my word; faithful, honest, and grounded in conviction. Help me keep my promises, even when I'm not obligated to, even when it could be inconvenient. Help me honor you when no one is watching. Let my "yes" be yes and my "no" be no, because you are a God who keeps his word. In Jesus's name, amen.

DAY 301

Overflowing Abundance

God will provide me with an abundance of all I need.

So your barns will be filled with plenty,
And your vats will overflow with new wine.

—PROVERBS 3:10

When He had stopped speaking, He said to Simon, "Launch out into the deep and let down your nets for a catch."
But Simon answered and said to Him, "Master, we have toiled all night and caught nothing; nevertheless at Your word I will let down the net." And when they had done this, they caught a great number of fish, and their net was breaking.

—LUKE 5:4-6

Dear Father God, not only do you always provide for my every need, but you also overflow my life with plenty. You rained fresh manna in the wilderness; you filled Simon's empty nets with so much fish the boat nearly sank. Thank you for sustaining me with daily bread and for the abundant flow of blessings on their way. You're a God who gives good gifts, and even when the abundance isn't material, you lavish me with love, strength, joy, and endurance. In Jesus's name, amen.

DAY 302

Good Things

Every gift is from God.

Every good gift and every perfect gift is from above, and comes down from the Father of lights, with whom there is no variation or shadow of turning.

—JAMES 1:17

Dear heavenly Father, thank you for being the giver of every good and perfect gift you have given me. In the small ordinary joys, in big loud celebrations and milestones, you are there! Your blessings encourage me to clear out the noise of everyday life and make room for you to move in my life. In every season, whether joyful or difficult, treasures are waiting, inviting me to step closer to you in faith. I want to experience the joy and gratitude of your bountiful love in every moment. Whether it's when I notice a sunset or a passing smile, I give thanks. In Jesus's name, amen.

DAY 303

Compassion

I want to have compassion like Jesus.

So Jesus had compassion and touched their eyes. And immediately their eyes received sight, and they followed Him.

—MATTHEW 20:34

Dear Jesus, when the two blind men cried out for your mercy and healing, you stopped to hear from them. Even if you may have heard their pleas, you directly asked them what they needed. And when they answered, their deepest desires to be cured, you gave them your heart and healed them. You demonstrate that you are here for me, have compassion for what I want, and offer wholeness. Will you show me the same tenderness I can extend to others? In your holy name, amen.

DAY 304

Lead by Example

I want to be a good teacher to those I lead.

Likewise, exhort the young men to be sober-minded, in all things showing yourself *to be* a pattern of good works; in doctrine *showing* integrity, reverence, incorruptibility, sound speech that cannot be condemned, that one who is an opponent may be ashamed, having nothing evil to say of you.

—TITUS 2:6-8

Dear Father God, I am so grateful for the people you placed in my life that taught me how to live a life that honors you. Their generosity and attitudes have a lasting impression and helped form who I am today. I am grateful for their edifying influence—but more importantly, it inspires me to be an encouraging confidant to others in the same way. I pray that my posture in my relationships can reflect the integrity and reverence you delight in—may my interactions with others uplift them. Use my gifts and strengths to be of service to others, even if it's not in visible leadership roles. In Jesus's name, amen.

DAY 305

God's Perfect Patience

I long to be patient like God the Father.

The Lord is not slack concerning *His* promise, as some count slackness, but is longsuffering toward us, not willing that any should perish but that all should come to repentance.

—2 PETER 3:9

Dear heavenly Father, just as you were patient with the Israelites in the wilderness when they doubted you and grumbled, you extend that same patience to me. Like the Israelites, I forget what you've done, complain, and overlook the blessings I've received. Yet you give me space to grow and lovingly wait for me to come to repentance when I make mistakes, thank you. In Jesus's name, amen.

DAY 306

Strength to Wait Well

Waiting on the Lord increases my strength.

But those who wait on the LORD
Shall renew *their* strength;
They shall mount up with wings like eagles,
They shall run and not be weary,
They shall walk and not faint.

—ISAIAH 40:31

"Watch and pray, lest you enter into temptation. The spirit indeed *is* willing, but the flesh *is* weak."

—MATTHEW 26:41

Dear God, waiting can be hard. When I don't know what you're doing behind the scenes, my flesh gets restless. I'm tempted to rush ahead of you and force what I want to happen. But you're so patient with me. Thank you for renewing my strength day after day as I wait on you. Help me wait well to trust your timing, seek you in prayer, and listen for the Holy Spirit's leading. What you have for me is worth the wait. In Jesus's name, amen.

DAY 307

No Greater Love

Nothing compares to your unwavering love.

And now abide faith, hope, love, these three; but the greatest of these *is* love.

—1 CORINTHIANS 13:13

Dear God, your love is so great, it has no limits and never fails. I could never fully grasp the depth of it, but I know it's the only supply that truly satisfies the deepest parts of my heart. Everything you do is out of your love for me. I've chased approval, success, and relationships, but nothing compares to your unwavering love. Remind me of this whenever I'm tempted to chase after lesser things. In Jesus's name, amen.

DAY 308

Clean My Heart

I want a pure heart in all things.

Draw near to God and He will draw near to you. Cleanse *your* hands, *you* sinners; and purify *your* hearts, *you* double-minded. Lament and mourn and weep! Let your laughter be turned to mourning and *your* joy to gloom. Humble yourselves in the sight of the Lord, and He will lift you up.

—JAMES 4:8-10

Dear God, purify and change my heart to love what you love and to lose all desire for anything that draws me away from you. Transform me to see your children and circumstances through your eyes. Give me a heart that is undivided, one that loves you supremely and seeks to reflect you in every interaction. Let my motivations be pure and rooted in love for you. In Jesus's name, amen.

DAY 309

Divine Protection

The Lord is with me through times of loss.

And I give them eternal life, and they shall never perish; neither shall anyone snatch them out of My hand. My Father, who has given *them* to Me, is greater than all; and no one is able to snatch *them* out of My Father's hand.

—JOHN 10:28-29

Dear heavenly Father, I'm discouraged when things don't go the way I hope or plan. When a dream I have doesn't come to pass, help me remember that your ways are better than mine, even when I don't understand them (Isaiah 55:9). Help me trust that what feels like a derailment might be a detour toward your divine protection. Remind me that your plans for my life are good so that I don't dwell on the plans of what could have been. In Jesus's name, amen.

DAY 310

Living in the Present

I want to live in the moment.

Therefore do not worry about tomorrow, for tomorrow will worry about its own things. Sufficient for the day *is* its own trouble.

—MATTHEW 6:34

Dear God, when I have moments of total belief in knowing that you are the God of all things, my heart feels relief and I feel content. Help me remember this feeling when I start replaying my past, worrying about the future, overthinking each step, or get distracted by the world and begin to overlook the life you've given me. Help me notice when your Spirit is whispering to me, set me on course so I can give my attention and presence to fully love my family, friends, and others in each moment spent with them. Keep me in the presence of Jesus. In Jesus's name, amen.

DAY 311

Rescued from the Pit

Depression is from the enemy.

He also brought me up out of a horrible pit,
Out of the miry clay,
And set my feet upon a rock,
And established my steps.

—PSALM 40:2

Dear Lord, I can fall into hopelessness and be desperate for any peace to cling to. When I'm in that place, I have the choice to reach out for you. Pull me out of the pit of despair. When the enemy whispers condemnation, let your unwavering love silence the lies that you've abandoned me or that I'm beyond repair. Anchor me in this truth—that I can put my hope in you alone. In Jesus's name, amen.

DAY 312

Comforted in Pain

When nothing will take away the pain of grief, I know God is still with me.

"Though I speak, my grief is not relieved;
And *if* I remain silent, how am I eased?"

—JOB 16:6

Dear heavenly Father, sometimes I feel like Job. No matter what I do, I find no relief from my pain. I don't always know what to do with my grief, and the loss is too heavy and deep to carry. But I know I can bring it to you, just as Jesus did as he was getting ready to go to the cross. In my sorrow, you are my only comfort. In Jesus's name, amen.

DAY 313

Beauty for Ashes

God trades me ashes for beauty.

"To console those who mourn in Zion,
To give them beauty for ashes,
The oil of joy for mourning,
The garment of praise for the spirit of heaviness;
That they may be called trees of righteousness,
The planting of the LORD, that He may be glorified."

—ISAIAH 61:3

Dear Father God, I am so thankful I can bring you the ashes of my life and you turn them into beauty. You trade mourning for joy and a spirit of heaviness for praise. You help me to always stay rooted in you, so that I can experience all the beauty in this life. I thank you that I can give you all the negative things in my life and you make them new and beautiful. In Jesus's name, amen.

DAY 314

Prayer for Ministry Leaders

May the Lord guide the shepherds of their flocks.

My brethren, let not many of you become teachers, knowing that we shall receive a stricter judgment.

—JAMES 3:1

Dear God, ministry leaders who shepherd your flock are at the front lines of serving our faith communities. Please guard their hearts from being led astray, discouragement, and falling into immorality. Raise up our brothers and sisters who can support them and share their load. Give them wisdom to serve the body of Christ and have a positive influence on our communities in ways that glorify you. Anchor them in your word and refresh them with your Spirit. In Jesus's name, amen.

DAY 315

Rejoice in the Future

I rejoice in what's ahead!

Strength and honor *are* her clothing;
She shall rejoice in time to come.

—PROVERBS 31:25

Dear God, thank you for allowing me to step into today clothed in your strength and honor. I can walk forward without any fear of the future, trusting that everything works together for good to those who love you (Romans 8:28). You complete the good work you've begun in me because you are faithful. I place my future in your hands, knowing you are the Creator of my story. In Jesus's name, amen.

DAY 316

Arise and Shine

The glory of the Lord is upon me.

Arise, shine;
For your light has come!
And the glory of the LORD is risen upon you.

—ISAIAH 60:1

Dear heavenly Father, because of your light, I do not have to walk in darkness, disconnected from your truth and love. Each day, you renew my strength and stir new desires in me, so that I can't help but shine. As I stand amazed in your presence, you show me the things I can bring into your light. You cleanse and free me from the darkness. Let your light reach the darkest places of my heart, reminding me that everything can be redeemed, healed, and made whole. In Jesus's name, amen.

DAY 317

Expect the Unexpected

My hope is in the unseen, not the seen.

For we were saved in this hope, but hope that is seen is not hope; for why does one still hope for what he sees? But if we hope for what we do not see, we eagerly wait for *it* with perseverance.

—ROMANS 8:24-25

Dear heavenly Father, It can be easier to place my hope in the tangible things that are in front of me, but faith doesn't work that way. Increase my faith when I have no idea how things will work out. You work in my life in unexpected ways like when I receive a check just in time to pay the bills, or experience miraculous healing. Keep my hope on fire, and may I trust in what you are doing even when I don't see it. In Jesus's name, amen.

DAY 318

Loving My Enemies

We are called to love others.

But I say to you, love your enemies, bless those who curse you, do good to those who hate you, and pray for those who spitefully use you and persecute you, that you may be sons of your Father in heaven; for He makes His sun rise on the evil and on the good, and sends rain on the just and on the unjust.

—MATTHEW 5:44-45

Dear God, resentment can build and I find I want to keep score when I am hurt by others. I want acknowledgment for their offense and validation for my hurt. But your word shows that even when Jesus was mocked, rejected, and betrayed, still he said, "Father, forgive them." Soften my heart to release my bitterness, forgive me when I speak out of spite, and give me a forgiving heart because you remind me that loving others shows them the mercy that reflects your heart. In Jesus's name, amen.

DAY 319

Holy Anger

Jesus displayed righteous anger.

Then Jesus went into the temple of God and drove out all those who bought and sold in the temple, and overturned the tables of the money changers and the seats of those who sold doves. And He said to them, "It is written, 'My house shall be called a house of prayer,' but you have made it a 'den of thieves.'"

—MATTHEW 21:12-13

Dear God, the anger I often feel is a human anger that stirs up outrage and resentment in my heart. But when Jesus showed anger, it was always righteous. Help me to have a heart like yours—fuel a righteous anger for meaningful change and transform it to compassion and not bitterness when I see others getting hurt and suffering injustice. Give me the wisdom to know when to speak up or act. In Jesus's name, amen.

DAY 320

Changing Seasons

I don't want to fear change.

Jesus Christ *is* the same yesterday, today, and forever.

—HEBREWS 13:8

Dear Lord, changes in this life approach like a tidal wave; some I see coming and some completely blindside me. In this season of transition, I worry I can't handle what's to come but you invite me to trust you. Remind me that every transition holds space for growth and opens doors for me to step into the new purpose that you've already prepared for the next season. Help me to rejoice and meet every change with faith instead of fear. I look forward to what you're doing. In Jesus's name, amen.

DAY 321

Courageous Leadership

Make me a courageous leader.

"Have I not commanded you? Be strong and of good courage; do not be afraid, nor be dismayed, for the Lord your God *is* with you wherever you go."

—JOSHUA 1:9

Dear Father God, the best leaders in the Bible were not those trying to seek positions of leadership but were called and equipped by you. My strength and courage don't come from myself, but from your presence in my life. Give me courage to face the giants in my life in the way David confronted his. You are always with me no matter where I go. In Jesus's name, amen.

DAY 322

A Unique Calling

God set me apart.

"Before I formed you in the womb I knew you;
Before you were born I sanctified you;
I ordained you a prophet to the nations."

—JEREMIAH 1:5

Dear God, you have prepared me for a purpose, and created me uniquely, different from each one of your children. You knitted me in the womb of my mother with exactly the gifts I need to walk out into my unique calling you've set me apart for. Even with this truth, I can stumble—not realizing how deeply you know me and want to know me more. I seek to nurture an intimate bond with you, to be secure in being seen and known by you. In Jesus's name, amen.

DAY 323

Believe in the One He Sent

Because of Jesus, I am worthy.

Then they said to Him, "What shall we do, that we may work the works of God?"
Jesus answered and said to them, "This is the work of God, that you believe in Him whom He sent."

—JOHN 6:28–29

Dear Lord Jesus, I find myself trying to do more to feel worthy, for approval. But the only thing you ask of me is to believe in you. Because of your sacrifice on the cross, I belong in your Kingdom and my position in heaven is secure, not through what I've done. Because of that, my soul can rest and I thank you forever for your sacrifice. In your powerful name, amen.

DAY 324

MERCY

God's mercy is forever.

Oh, give thanks to the LORD, for *He is* good!
For His mercy *endures* forever.

—PSALM 118:1

Dear Father God, I am so thankful to be a daughter of the Most High King (Psalm 82:6). I am undeserving of your mercy, and yet you freely give it. You are faithful, and your love will endure forever. In moments when I feel stuck or stagnant, I want to give thanks for each new mercy you pour on me. In Jesus's name, amen.

DAY 325

A HEART THAT DOESN'T GRUMBLE

Do everything without complaint.

Therefore do not cast away your confidence, which has great reward. For you have need of endurance, so that after you have done the will of God, you may receive the promise.

—HEBREWS 10:35-36

Dear heavenly Father, having faith entails living with intentionality in my words, thoughts, and actions. When I sink into hopelessness in difficult seasons, it's unclear how I will move forward, and I confess I'd sometimes rather remain in the heaviness because it feels easier to wallow in it. Thank you for never discounting my pains and challenges—instead, you hear me and carry my pain. Whatever circumstances life may pose, being a faithful child means to remain patient, content, and holding on to your word. When I struggle, I can lean on you and grow in patience. In Jesus's name, amen.

DAY 326

Telling the Truth

I want to share my faith with those around me, knowing the truth will set them free.

For the time will come when they will not endure sound doctrine, but according to their own desires, *because* they have itching ears, they will heap up for themselves teachers; and they will turn *their* ears away from the truth, and be turned aside to fables. But you be watchful in all things, endure afflictions, do the work of an evangelist, fulfill your ministry.

—2 TIMOTHY 4:3–5

Dear God, my heart longs for others to feel your unconditional love. Open the hearts of those who are ready to receive and encounter Jesus. Give me an urgency to share about your love without compromise and not water down anything that's hard to hear. Give me gentleness and kindness. Give me courage and boldness to share my faith. In Jesus's name, amen.

DAY 327

Perfect Peace

Perfect peace is birthed from trusting God.

You will keep *him* in perfect peace,
Whose mind *is* stayed *on You,*
Because he trusts in You.

—ISAIAH 26:3

Dear Lord, perfect peace doesn't come from perfect circumstances, it comes from trusting you. Just as Paul and Silas sang in prison, and Jesus calmed the storm with a word, remind me that peace is found in your presence, not in control. Even when life feels uncertain, draw my attention back to you when I'm tempted to focus on the storm instead of the One that calms it. Thank you for being steady, faithful, and by my side. I choose to rest in your peace today. In Jesus's name, amen.

DAY 328

Simple Gratitude

God is good, I am thankful!

Oh, give thanks to the Lord, for *He is* good!
For His mercy *endures* forever.

—1 CHRONICLES 16:34

Dear heavenly Father, I want to take some time today just to simply acknowledge your goodness. Your love is steady, and your mercy never runs out. You give us what we don't deserve, extending limitless forgiveness and restoring us. Thank you for showing me compassion and kindness when I need it the most. Thank you for the extraordinary blessings like the roof over my head to the ordinary joys like my daily bread. You are hope. In Jesus's name, amen.

DAY 329

As If I've Never Sinned

We are justified through God's grace.

For all have sinned and fall short of the glory of God, being justified freely by His grace through the redemption that is in Christ Jesus, whom God set forth as a propitiation by His blood, through faith, to demonstrate His righteousness, because in His forbearance God had passed over the sins that were previously committed, to demonstrate at the present time His righteousness, that He might be just and the justifier of the one who has faith in Jesus.

—ROMANS 3:23–26

Dear Father God, thank you for the sacrifice Jesus paid for every sin so I could stand before you as righteous. You justified me and treat me just as if I've never sinned. When I fail, I can look to you and remember your grace always covers me. My standing with you is secure because of your perfect love for me. You gave me a way to walk free from guilt because of your grace. In Jesus's name, amen.

DAY 330

He Waits for Me

Even if I walked away and denied the Lord, he would still love me.

He said to him the third time, "Simon, *son* of Jonah, do you love Me?" Peter was grieved because He said to him the third time, "Do you love Me?" And he said to Him, "Lord, You know all things; You know that I love You." Jesus said to him, "Feed My sheep."

—JOHN 21:17

Dear Father God, even after Peter betrayed Jesus three times, Jesus entrusts him to lead and care for his sheep. This exchange displays such a deep love, and the same love that is offered to us, though we are undeserving of it. But Jesus is there, willing, waiting to forgive and use us in mighty ways. This knowledge doesn't give me the freedom to keep drifting and denying you, but to believe and be assured in your vast love for me. Even when I make wrong choices, Jesus is still faithful and meets me where I am. In Jesus's name, amen.

DAY 331

Putting You First

I want to seek the Lord before anything else.

Jesus said to him, " 'You shall love the LORD your God with all your heart, with all your soul, and with all your mind.' This is *the* first and great commandment."

—MATTHEW 22:37-38

Dear Lord, instead of turning to seek you first, in the blink of an eye, I open my phone and am flooded with updates from every corner of the world. Give me a heart that longs for you above all else. Anchor me so that I may love you with my whole heart and mind, and nothing else competes with my love for you. This world is fleeting, but you and your steadfast love are eternal. In Jesus's name, amen.

DAY 332

Rooted in Christ

Like a tree, may my roots sink deep into your soil.

As you therefore have received Christ Jesus the Lord, so walk in Him, rooted and built up in Him and established in the faith, as you have been taught, abounding in it with thanksgiving.

—COLOSSIANS 2:6-7

Dear Lord, I want to be deeply rooted in you like a tree drawing life, strength, and sustenance from its roots. Just as a tree with severed roots cannot survive, I know I cannot thrive apart from you. Like the good soil in the parable of the sower, soften my heart to receive the nourishment of your word. Let it take deep root in me and satisfy my soul with what's lasting and eternal. In Jesus's name, amen.

DAY 333

Love Like Yours

I want to love with intention.

This is My commandment, that you love one another as I have loved you. Greater love has no one than this, than to lay down one's life for his friends.

—JOHN 15:12-13

Dear Father God, I want to love those around me with the same unconditional love that you have for your followers. I want to love fiercely with intention, always with a kind heart. I always want to treat others with the love that I would like to receive in return (Luke 6:31). Please work within me to make me intentional in my relationships. In Jesus's name, amen.

DAY 334

Equipped and Empowered to Serve

I am able to fulfill my calling because the Lord is with me.

But Moses said to God, "Who *am* I that I should go to Pharaoh, and that I should bring the children of Israel out of Egypt?" So He said, "I will certainly be with you. And this *shall be* a sign to you that I have sent you: When you have brought the people out of Egypt, you shall serve God on this mountain."

— EXODUS 3:11-12

Dear Lord, thank you for the great calling you've placed on my life not because I can do it on my own, but because you equip me. Thank you for entrusting me to fulfill your purposes here on earth. When the road gets difficult and I'm afraid I can't keep going, you never leave my side. You have given me everything I need to propel forward. When I doubt myself or don't always feel ready, you are always with me. In Jesus's name, amen.

DAY 335

High Upon a Rock

God is my refuge.

For in the time of trouble
He shall hide me in His pavilion;
In the secret place of His tabernacle
He shall hide me;
He shall set me high upon a rock.

—PSALM 27:5

Dear Lord, you are my refuge when I am in times of trouble. I can come to you and confess, regardless of my circumstances or what I have done—you always meet me with your loving-kindness. You are a good Father and though I may struggle in this life, you are there to guide me through it all and I will come out of those challenges stronger and capable of more joy because you were with me. Thank you for being a present Father. In Jesus's name, amen.

DAY 336

Redeem My Past

I long to be in the present, not stuck in the past.

"Do not remember the former things,
Nor consider the things of old.
Behold, I will do a new thing,
Now it shall spring forth;
Shall you not know it?
I will even make a road in the wilderness
And rivers in the desert."

—ISAIAH 43:18-19

"So I will restore to you the years that the swarming locust has eaten,
The crawling locust,
The consuming locust,
And the chewing locust,
My great army which I sent among you."

—JOEL 2:25

Dear God, I try to move forward, but I end up being reminded of what the "locusts" of my past have stolen, broken, or wasted. Expand my heart to stop replaying what cannot be changed from my past, give thanks for this present moment, and look forward to a bright future for me because you're writing a new story for my life. Restore everything I've lost and make me whole so your peace can shine through my life. In Jesus's name, amen.

DAY 337

Learning from Pain

God uses painful situations to draw me closer to him.

And *though* the Lord gives you
The bread of adversity and the water of affliction,
Yet your teachers will not be moved into a corner anymore,
But your eyes shall see your teachers.
Your ears shall hear a word behind you, saying,
"This *is* the way, walk in it,"
Whenever you turn to the right hand.
Or whenever you turn to the left.

—ISAIAH 30:20–21

Dear Father God, I come to you carrying weight I can't seem to shed free from. I don't always understand how you're working in me, and when I can't always see the purpose of my suffering, it shakes my faith. But you say my pain is never wasted. Even though I wouldn't choose to go through it, you use my pain to deepen my faith. Reveal to me that comfort is found only in you, relieve the burden of this season, and make me resilient. You are refining me. In Jesus's name, amen.

DAY 338

Bearing One Another's Burdens

Give me a heart for the people around me.

Bear one another's burdens, and so fulfill the law of Christ.

—GALATIANS 6:2

Dear God, sometimes I get so caught up in everything I have going on that I can be callous to what others around me may need. As you love me, I want to generously love others, become a trustworthy confidant, a present friend, a caring sister in faith. Reveal to me those in my life that need support and prayer, so I can help carry their burdens when they face challenges and hardships. In Jesus's name, amen.

DAY 339

A Heart of Offering

I want to give to God first.

"Bring all the tithes into the storehouse,
That there may be food in My house,
And try Me now in this,"
Says the LORD of hosts,
"If I will not open for you the windows of heaven
And pour out for you *such* blessing
That *there will* not *be room* enough *to receive it.*"

—MALACHI 3:10

Dear heavenly Father, you have freely given me all I have. Everything in this life is a gift from you. Give me a willing and generous heart—whether it's in the form of my money, time, or talents. As Jesus's disciples faithfully followed him, give my heart the same intentionality and dedication to you. Even when I wrestle with uncertainty or doubt, Jesus's faithfulness to your beloved disciples lights my path. In Jesus's name, amen.

DAY 340

Grace for the Humble

Humility and grace go hand in hand.

But He gives more grace. Therefore He says:
"God resists the proud,
But gives grace to the humble."

—JAMES 4:6

Dear Father God, humble me so I can receive all you have in this life for me. Guard my heart from pride, which keeps me from recognizing how deeply I need you. When I crave recognition and praise, remind me that I'm not here to build my own kingdom or make a name for myself. Jesus didn't seek to promote himself but only did what you called him to do. Your grace and favor are better than any applause this world can offer. In Jesus's name, amen.

DAY 341

CULTIVATE

I want to cultivate a spiritual environment.

Let the word of Christ dwell in you richly in all wisdom, teaching and admonishing one another in psalms and hymns and spiritual songs, singing with grace in your hearts to the Lord. And whatever you do in word or deed, *do* all in the name of the Lord Jesus, giving thanks to God the Father through Him.

—COLOSSIANS 3:16–17

Dear Father God, I want to cultivate a fertile environment in my life where your Holy Spirit is felt, your word comes to life, and hearts are drawn to you. When your word is dwelling at the the center of my life and guiding everything I do, you are shaping how I think, speak, and act. Help me nurture a heart environment that is brimming with praise and thanksgiving, to reflect your glory. In Jesus's name, amen.

DAY 342

GOD'S FAITHFULNESS

God's faithfulness never fails.

Through the LORD's mercies we are not consumed,
Because His compassions fail not.
They are new every morning;
Great *is* Your faithfulness.

—LAMENTATIONS 3:22–23

Dear heavenly Father, you stay faithful at each new day, no matter how much I fail. Even when I'm fickle or impatient, you remain steadfast and always show up when I need you. You don't delight in my pain, you invite me to lean on your unchanging love, rather than my own fluctuating feelings. Thank you for your new mercies every day. In Jesus's name, amen.

DAY 343

Wellspring of Life

Wisdom and understanding are a wellspring of life.

Understanding *is* a wellspring of life to him who has it.
But the correction of fools *is* folly.

The heart of the wise teaches his mouth,
And adds learning to his lips.

—PROVERBS 16:22–23

Dear Lord, grant me wisdom not only in my actions, but also in the words I speak. I don't want to be wise in my own eyes or lean on worldly understanding. Your wisdom is pure and life-giving. Keep my heart humble and give me a deep desire to get to know you. May your wisdom overflow in my life like a wellspring. In Jesus's name, amen.

DAY 344

A Gentle Spirit

Give me a gentle spirit, Lord.

I, therefore, the prisoner of the Lord, beseech you to walk worthy of the calling with which you were called, with all lowliness and gentleness, with longsuffering, bearing with one another in love.

—EPHESIANS 4:1–2

Dear Father God, grow a gentle spirit in me that reflects your love and compassion. Even when I'm feeling overwhelmed or dealing with unmet expectations, help me release my tendency to control or impose my own will onto others or situations. I choose your light in a world that often values dominance over gentleness. In Jesus's name, amen.

DAY 345

You Meet Me in the Ordinary

God knows where I am and what I need.

Jesus said to them, "Come *and* eat breakfast." Yet none of the disciples dared ask Him, "Who are You?"—knowing that it was the Lord. Jesus then came and took the bread and gave it to them, and likewise the fish.

—JOHN 21:12-13

Now it came to pass, as He sat at the table with them, that He took bread, blessed and broke *it*, and gave it to them. Then their eyes were opened and they knew Him; and He vanished from their sight.
And they said to one another, "Did not our heart burn within us while He talked with us on the road, and while He opened the Scriptures to us?"

—LUKE 24:30-32

Dear Lord Jesus, after your disciples were at sea and caught nothing, you were there to meet them and commanded them to try again when they caught a net full of fish. You broke bread and invited them to share a meal. Just as you were there with your disciples at each moment of need, you know exactly where to meet me and fulfill my need. You provide nourishment and give me rest. It's not only in the desperate dramatic moments that I meet you, it's in the ordinary moments. At any moment that can easily be overlooked, you are intimately there with me, witnessing each small detail, so that I am known by you. I can sit and rest with you by my side. Thank you, amen.

DAY 346

A Supernatural Love

I want to love like Jesus.

And above all things have fervent love for one another, for "love will cover a multitude of sins."

—1 PETER 4:8

Dear heavenly Father, thank you for showing me perfect love through Jesus. Encountering heartache, struggles, and challenges makes it easy to develop a calloused heart and it becomes hard to receive and give love. Heal the places in my heart that have been wounded from betrayal and disappointment. Transform my heart to always choose love even when loving others doesn't always come naturally, because it's your love that ultimately flows through me. In Jesus's name, amen.

DAY 347

Perseverance Toward Victory

I will persevere and run the race the Lord has set before me.

Therefore we also, since we are surrounded by so great a cloud of witnesses, let us lay aside every weight, and the sin which so easily ensnares *us*, and let us run with endurance the race that is set before us, looking unto Jesus, the author and finisher of *our* faith, who for the joy that was set before Him endured the cross, despising the shame, and has sat down at the right hand of the throne of God.

—HEBREWS 12:1-2

Dear heavenly Father, you have given me a race to run, one that requires endurance and faith. Reveal to me anything hindering my pace. I desire to lay aside every weight and distraction so I can run freely, to the author and finisher of my faith. When I grow weary, remind me that the victory is already mine through Christ! I want to step forward in faith without any hesitation. In Jesus's name, amen.

DAY 348

Obedience Unlocks Blessings

Blessings are birthed from obedience.

But be doers of the word, and not hearers only, deceiving yourselves. For if anyone is a hearer of the word and not a doer, he is like a man observing his natural face in a mirror; for he observes himself, goes away, and immediately forgets what kind of man he was. But he who looks into the perfect law of liberty and continues *in it*, and is not a forgetful hearer but a doer of the work, this one will be blessed in what he does.

—JAMES 1:22–25

Dear Lord, your word tells me that blessings are birthed from when I am obedient. It's not because you reward my performance transactionally, but because your ways lead to life. Remind me that obeying you means I'm aligning myself with a path that is secure and fruitful. Give me strength to follow your commands. In Jesus's name, amen.

DAY 349

Freedom in Christ

Christ set me free from the bondage of sin.

Stand fast therefore in the liberty by which Christ has made us free, and do not be entangled again with a yoke of bondage.

—GALATIANS 5:1

Dear heavenly Father, thank you for sending your Son to die on the cross for my sins and be resurrected on the third day. Jesus Christ is the one who made a way for me, he is the one who set me free from the bondage of sin. Give me pause to slow down and delight in your goodness. I pray I never lose my sense of wonder in you. In Jesus's name, amen.

DAY 350

Glory

I desire to bear good fruit.

"For a good tree does not bear bad fruit, nor does a bad tree bear good fruit. For every tree is known by its own fruit. For *men* do not gather figs from thorns, nor do they gather grapes from a bramble bush."

—LUKE 6:43-44

Father God, how I act, speak, live, and treat others comes from the inside. Till the soil of my heart, weed out lies, shame, fear, anger, and harshness. Nourish my soul with nutrients filled with the fruits of the Holy Spirit and plant seeds of your word and will so that I may bear good fruit in abundance that reflects your character and nature! In Jesus's name, amen.

DAY 351

Called to Create

Everything was created by a creative God.

In the beginning God created the heavens and the earth.

—GENESIS 1:1

Dear heavenly Father, you are the ultimate Creator. You formed the heavens, the earth, and every living thing with beauty and purpose. Sometimes I wonder if my creativity matters, but you remind me it reflects your image. You didn't just make what was necessary, you made what was beautiful. Thank you for placing creativity in me. Help me create boldly, knowing it's an important part of my calling. In Jesus's name, amen.

DAY 352

Unashamed of the Truth

May I never be ashamed of the work of the gospel.

In You, O LORD, I put my trust;
Let me never be ashamed;
Deliver me in Your righteousness.

—PSALM 31:1

Dear God, you are my rock, my shield, and my help. I put all my faith and trust in you. Thank you for the gift of the Good News that through Jesus's death and resurrection, I have victory over sin and am made new. Just like Jesus was unashamed to follow your will, may my life reflect the power of the gospel. When I'm filled with doubt and I feel surrounded by darkness, fill me with your Spirit, assure my each step on your path. In Jesus's name, amen.

DAY 353

Clothed in Strength and Honor

I want to be clothed in strength, honor, wisdom, and kindness with no fear of the future.

But put on the Lord Jesus Christ, and make no provision for the flesh, to *fulfill* its lusts.

—ROMANS 13:14

Dear Lord, make me bold and courageous, yet gentle and kind, always honoring others like Jesus. Even though he was the King of Kings and he had every right to be served, Jesus took the lowest place and washed his disciples' feet. Even when I don't execute it perfectly, let me be a daughter who speaks life-giving words to encourage others and a willingness to put others first, and the vigilance to guard her own heart. In Jesus's name, amen.

DAY 354

By Bread Alone

May you provide your word as a daily bread to me.

But He answered and said, "It is written, 'Man shall not live by bread alone, but by every word that proceeds from the mouth of God.'"

—MATTHEW 4:4

Dear Jesus, no matter what was happening, you turned to God's Word to sustain you while you were here on earth, whether you were hungry, tired, or tempted. When I'm feeling emotionally drained or overwhelmed, I reach for temporary comfort like food, distractions, or advice that might not align with your word. But none of that satisfies me. Help me see your word as my daily bread that nourishes, heals, and restores my soul. In your name, amen.

DAY 355

Transformed by Truth

Word before world.

Then He said to *them* all, "If anyone desires to come after Me, let him deny himself, and take up his cross daily, and follow Me."

—LUKE 9:23

Dear God, you uniquely made me who I am. But there are influences I've picked up from the world that are not of you. Cleanse my mind from the lies I've come to believe about myself, others, or even you. Through immersing myself in the Word, teach me so I may see everything through your eyes with clarity and certainty. Anchor me in truth and conform me to the image of Jesus and not the world. In Jesus's name, amen.

DAY 356

Strength in Surrender

I am strong because the Lord is strong.

I can do all things through Christ who strengthens me.

—PHILIPPIANS 4:13

Dear Lord, when I try to be strong on my own, I'm left worn and empty. On my own, I'm weak. But you invite me to find strength in your presence—true strength doesn't come from striving but from surrender. I surrender my fears, the pressure to have it all together, and my need to control what's ahead. Transform me so I act within the strength only you can give me in Christ. In Jesus's name, amen.

DAY 357

Jesus Will Provide

In our time of need, he provides what we need.

Then He took the five loaves and the two fish, and looking up to heaven, He blessed and broke them, and gave *them* to the disciples to set before the multitude. So they all ate and were filled, and twelve baskets of the leftover fragments were taken up by them.

—LUKE 9:16-17

Dear God, as a daughter in Christ, I bear my earthly responsibilities with both pride and joy. It fills my life when I can be a part of my church's ministry, a good neighbor to my community, a providing caregiver, a caring confidant. But I can feel inadequate to fulfill them well. In these moments, remind me that Jesus was there when the disciples couldn't feed the five thousand. Jesus answered with a miracle. I simply need to seek your help! Make room in my heart so Jesus can step in and do the unimaginable. In Jesus's name, amen.

DAY 358

Our Comforter

God is my comforter in times of trouble.

Yea, though I walk through the valley of the shadow of death,
I will fear no evil;
For You *are* with me;
Your rod and Your staff, they comfort me.

—PSALM 23:4

Dear heavenly Father, you are my comforter in times of trouble—you're always here for me, even when I walk through the darkest of times and my path is unsteady. I truly am never alone. In Jesus's name, amen.

DAY 359

Overcoming People Pleasing

I long to please God, not people.

But Jesus did not commit Himself to them, because He knew all *men*, and had no need that anyone should testify of man, for He knew what was in man.

—JOHN 2:24-25

For do I now persuade men, or God? Or do I seek to please men? For if I still pleased men, I would not be a bondservant of Christ.

—GALATIANS 1:10

Dear Jesus, thank you for showing me what it looks like to put God first. I struggle with wanting to please others, receiving approval from others, and worry about hurting or offending others. Thank you for giving me a big heart but also for holding a mirror up for me to recognize my tendencies. Give me the strength to rely on you rather than putting my hopes and expectations on the relationships in my life. When I fear disappointing others and need validation, center me on being obedient to what you've called me for, as I have nothing to fear. In your name, amen.

DAY 360

Believing God for the Impossible

Nothing is impossible for God.

But Jesus looked at *them* and said to them, "With men this is impossible, but with God all things are possible."

—MATTHEW 19:26

Dear Jesus, sometimes situations in life feel hopeless and beyond repair. But this is a lie because with you, nothing is impossible. You walked on water, healed the blind, and turned water into wine. Even the winds and waves obeyed you. The greatest miracle, one only possible through you, is that you delivered me from sin. Remind me when I face seemingly impossible circumstances that God specializes in the impossible. In your name, amen.

DAY 361

From Repentance to Freedom

The Holy Spirit convicts.

For godly sorrow produces repentance *leading* to salvation, not to be regretted; but the sorrow of the world produces death.

—2 CORINTHIANS 7:10

Dear Father God, Peter betrayed Jesus three times, but through his awakening, he repented for his sin and turned away from his worldly ways. When I sin, I turn to self-pity, guilt, or shame. But you've given us the gift of faith as an invitation to turn away from brokenness, and to step into wholeness. Give me the boldness to quickly repent and experience your forgiveness, to fully encounter confession as a path to freedom and transformation. In Jesus's name, amen.

DAY 362

Beautifully Made

I am fearfully and wonderfully made.

For You formed my inward parts;
You covered me in my mother's womb.
I will praise You, for I am fearfully *and* wonderfully made . . .

—PSALM 139:13–14

Dear heavenly Father, I'm so grateful for this body you've given me and the life you've blessed me with. The fact that I'm here is a miracle, and everything about me was purposefully formed by you. Help me see myself how you see me. You made me beautiful—simply because I'm yours. My body reflects your creativity and craftsmanship. In Jesus's name, amen.

DAY 363

Abide with Jesus

Help me slow down and listen for the Holy Spirit.

Abide in Me, and I in you. As the branch cannot bear fruit of itself, unless it abides in the vine, neither can you, unless you abide in Me.

—JOHN 15:4

Dear Lord, oftentimes I think I'm staying connected in you, but I've actually disconnected. I intend to be present with you, but my mind is elsewhere, distracted, rushing, overwhelmed. You speak to me daily, but I'm not always ready to receive it. I don't want to be like those who followed Jesus and stopped abiding when things got hard. Help me slow down to listen to the voice of the Holy Spirit and receive what you have for me each day. In Jesus's name, amen.

DAY 364

Joy in the Morning

When I am filled with sadness, I have peace knowing that sadness will not remain forever.

A time to weep,
And a time to laugh;
A time to mourn,
And a time to dance.

—ECCLESIASTES 3:4

Dear Lord, when grief feels overwhelming, remind me it's okay—even necessary—to mourn. You give me the permission to grieve as a part of healing. Thank you for promising that one day, all pain and sorrow will be gone. Until then, fill me with your love and peace. Let me feel your presence as you sit with me in the sadness and hear my sorrows. Remind me that this grief will not last forever and you'll give me joy in the morning. In Jesus's name, amen.

DAY 365

An Abundant Life

Make me like a tree planted in the river of life.

Blessed *is* the man
Who walks not in the counsel of the ungodly,
Nor stands in the path of sinners,
Nor sits in the seat of the scornful;
But his delight *is* in the law of the LORD,
And in His law he meditates day and night.
He shall be like a tree
Planted by the rivers of water,
That brings forth its fruit in its season,
Whose leaf also shall not wither;
And whatever he does shall prosper.

—PSALM 1:1–3

Dear heavenly Father, when I picture a faithful life, I often picture a garden always in bloom—flourishing with beauty, joy, and fruit. But the truth is, I'm human, and the weeds of worry, distraction, and sin begin to choke out the good things growing in my garden. I pray that your Holy Spirit will help me to keep you at the center of my life and delight in your word day and night. As I'm planted in your presence, may my life produce fruit that brings you glory. In Jesus's name, amen.

ACKNOWLEDGMENTS

As followers of Christ, I don't believe we are ever called to do anything completely alone. God calls us to community with both him and other believers. It has been thanks to so many people that I was able to see my first book traditionally published.

To Tim, my love, you have always believed in me, even when I haven't believed in myself. You sat with me and helped me dream up topics, helped me solidify my thoughts and pick out verses—you helped this book come to life right along with me. You have been my greatest support here on earth, and I am so thankful that you choose me time and time again. I am grateful to be doing life with you, glorifying the Lord and doing Kingdom work together. I love you to the moon and back.

To Titus and Wesley, my sweet boys. It is likely that neither of you will remember the time I wrote my first traditionally published book. The time we spent on the floor, Wesley on tummy time, Titus playing with trains, and me on my computer writing out prayers when I had a moment to spare. You have walked this road with me, whether you ever know it or not. Thank you for being my greatest inspiration, for being my greatest life lessons, and for being the greatest gifts from the heavenly Father. Being your mom is my ultimate honor and I will love you forever, my whole life.

To my mom, Julie, whose response was truly priceless when I told her I was going to be a published author—"I knew you could do it!" My dream to be published has been something I have carried with me since I was 14, and you have now had the opportunity to watch that dream come to fruition before our very eyes. Thank you for always believing in me and for all of the sacrifices you made to make my dreams a reality throughout the whole of my life. Your sacrifices never went unnoticed, not by me, and not by the God who created you.

To my family and friends who supported me as I shared my dreams of writing this book, as they checked in to see how writing was coming along, and as they supported me along the way—you know who you are. Thank you.

To Tahra and Caroline, I wouldn't be here today without the two of you championing me for the writing of this book, encouraging me to keep going, and helping me see one of my biggest dreams come to fruition through the penning of this book. You two are treasures within the publishing community, and I am so grateful I had the opportunity to work with both of you through this process.

To Helen, your support on this piece has been insurmountable. I have been continuously grateful for every suggestion you have made to make this project the absolute best that it could be. I wouldn't have been able to watch this book come to life without your help.

To Yahweh. To the one who created my inmost being, who knit me together in my mother's womb, and who first gave me the desire to pick up a pen and write. Thank you, Lord, for using me as your vessel. I am so imperfect, filled with so many flaws, and yet, you chose to use me. I am humbled and in awe. I love you, Lord. This book is all for you and your glory.

ABOUT THE AUTHOR

Alexis Kanode is a Christian coach, a creative, and an entrepreneur known for her love for Christ and her encouragement for Christian women and other mothers. She is the founder of Garden of Glory Co, a faith-based online shop, and has written self-published Bible studies and devotionals, including *Closer: Approaching the Throne of Grace with Confidence.* She leads a quiet life with her husband, Tim, and two boys in the foothills of Pennsylvania. Find out more at instagram.com/alexiskanode.

ANCHOR YOUR HEART
in God's unwavering and
unconditional love for you
with this guided prayer
journal filled with devotions,
prompts, and more

A TENDER, LOVING
Christian devotional
offering weekly prayers
and faith-based practices
to heal and find a path
toward a forgiving heart

www.zeitgeistpublishing.com

Hi there,

We hope you enjoyed *Pray with Jesus*. If you have any questions or concerns about your book, or have received a damaged copy, please contact customerservice@penguinrandomhouse.com. We're here and happy to help.

Also, please consider writing a review on your favorite retailer's website to let others know what you thought of the book!

Sincerely,

The Zeitgeist Team